ANDREW T. LE PEAU

AND PHYLLIS J. LE PEAU

A Deeper Look at
JAMES

NINE SESSIONS FOR GROUPS AND INDIVIDUALS

FAITH THAT WORKS

LifeGuide®
IN DEPTH
BIBLE STUDIES

IVP Connect
An imprint of InterVarsity Press
Downers Grove, Illinois

InterVarsity Press
P.O. Box 1400, Downers Grove, IL 60515-1426
World Wide Web: www.ivpress.com
E-mail: email@ivpress.com

Design: Cindy Kiple
Images: © rusm/iStockphoto

ISBN 978-0-8308-3101-2 (print)

Printed in the United States of America ∞

P	24	23	22	21	20	19	18	17	16	15	14	13	12	11	10	9	8	7	6	5	4	3	2	1
Y	34	33	32	31	30	29	28	27	26	25	24	23	22	21	20	19	18	17	16	15	14	13		

CONTENTS

INTRODUCTION

Faith That Works

he New Testament letter of James is one of the most appreciated and most troubling books of the New Testament. People love its down-to-earth practicality. There's no erudite theology or philosophy here. No sir! James's focus is on living the Christian life. His Proverbs-like conciseness is clear and direct. In fact, James is very pointed at times in his criticisms of the rich, the argumentative and those who are teachers.

On the other hand, readers find James frustrating and confusing. He does not seem to line up with Paul's teaching on salvation by faith. In fact, when he says faith without works is dead, he seems to be saying the opposite of Paul.

One of the other curious characteristics about the letter of James is that very little is said about Jesus. In fact, Jesus is only mentioned by name twice in the letter—in 1:1 ("the Lord Jesus Christ") and 2:1 ("our glorious Lord Jesus Christ"). "The Lord" is mentioned thirteen other times in the letter, but each of these (with the exception of 5:7-8) could be general references to God or God the Father rather than to Jesus.

Since every other book of the New Testament mentions Jesus dozens and dozens of times, this difference in James's letter is rather conspicuous. It is also curious because tradition has it that the James who wrote the letter was in fact the half-brother of Jesus. (There are four people named James in the New Testament. Two were apostles [see Matthew 10:2-4]. Another was the father of the apostle Judas [not Iscariot; see Luke 6:16]. And then there is the brother of Jesus who, though he did not accept Jesus' authority before the resurrection,

became the head of the church in Jerusalem [see Matthew 13:55 and Acts 12:17; 15:13].) Some speculate that James deliberately downplays his blood relationship to the Savior so as not to fall victim to the arrogance of speech he condemns in his letter.

In any case, while explicit reference to Jesus is minimal in the letter, the influence of Jesus is profound and pervasive. As we will see in the course of this book, Jesus' words in the Gospel of Matthew and in the Sermon on the Mount in particular strongly affected James and his letter. We don't know if James had a copy of the Gospel of Matthew as he wrote, but certainly he knew the oral tradition of the Sermon on the Mount that had been passed down through the church in the decades between Jesus' death and the writing of the various New Testament books. The chart "Comparing James and Sermon on the Mount" on the next page offers a sampling of what we will see.

James shows how he has integrated the teaching of Jesus into his own life, thought and instruction to the church in Jerusalem where he was the leader (Acts 12:17; 15:12-23; Galatians 1:19; 2:9). His leadership in the church ultimately resulted in his death by stoning in A.D. 62. This was part of the ongoing persecution of the infant church that had begun in Acts 7–8 with the stoning of Stephen, probably no later than A.D. 40. That the letter is addressed to "the twelve tribes scattered among the nations" (1:1) indicates not only that this letter was likely intended to circulate among the various Christian communities in the Mediterranean basin, but also that these early Christians were no strangers to persecution and its results.

Comparing James and Sermon on the Mount

LETTER OF JAMES	SERMON ON THE MOUNT
James 1:2, 12 Consider it pure joy, my brothers and sisters, whenever you face trials of many kinds. . . . Blessed is the one who perseveres under trial because, having stood the test, that person will receive the crown of life that the Lord has promised to those who love him.	**Matthew 5:11-12** "Blessed are you when people insult you, persecute you and falsely say all kinds of evil against you because of me. Rejoice and be glad, because great is your reward in heaven, for in the same way they persecuted the prophets who were before you."
James 1:5-6 If any of you lacks wisdom, you should ask God, who gives generously to all without finding fault, and it will be given to you. But when you ask, you must believe and not doubt, because the one who doubts is like a wave of the sea, blown and tossed by the wind.	**Matthew 7:7-8** "Ask and it will be given to you; seek and you will find; knock and the door will be opened to you. For everyone who asks receives; the one who seeks finds; and to the one who knocks, the door will be opened."
James 1:10 But the rich should take pride in their humiliation—since they will pass away like a wild flower.	**Matthew 6:30** "If that is how God clothes the grass of the field, which is here today and tomorrow is thrown into the fire, will he not much more clothe you—you of little faith?"
James 1:13 When tempted, no one should say, "God is tempting me." For God cannot be tempted by evil, nor does he tempt anyone.	**Matthew 6:13** "And lead us not into temptation, but deliver us from the evil one."
James 1:19 Everyone should be . . . slow to speak.	**Matthew 5:34-37** "But I tell you, do not swear an oath at all: either by heaven, for it is God's throne; or by the earth, for it is his footstool. . . . All you need to say is simply 'Yes' or 'No'; anything beyond this comes from the evil one."
James 1:19 Everyone should be . . . slow to become angry.	**Matthew 5:21-22** "You have heard that it was said to the people long ago, 'You shall not murder, and anyone who murders will be subject to judgment.' But I tell you that anyone who is angry with a brother or sister will be subject to judgment."
James 1:22 Do not merely listen to the word, and so deceive yourselves. Do what it says.	**Matthew 7:21, 24** "Not everyone who says to me, 'Lord, Lord,' will enter the kingdom of heaven, but only the one who does the will of my Father who is in heaven." "Therefore everyone who hears these words of mine and puts them into practice is like a wise man who built his house on the rock."
James 2:4 Have you not discriminated among yourselves and become judges with evil thoughts?	**Matthew 7:1-2** "Do not judge, or you too will be judged. For in the same way you judge others, you will be judged, and with the measure you use, it will be measured to you."

Comparing James and Sermon on the Mount (Continued)

LETTER OF JAMES	SERMON ON THE MOUNT
James 2:5 Has not God chosen those who are poor in the eyes of the world to be rich in faith and to inherit the kingdom he promised those who love him?	**Matthew 5:3, 5** "Blessed are the poor in spirit, for theirs is the kingdom of heaven. . . . Blessed are the meek, for they will inherit the earth."
James 2:10-11 For whoever keeps the whole law and yet stumbles at just one point is guilty of breaking all of it. For he who said, "You shall not commit adultery," also said, "You shall not murder." If you do not commit adultery but do commit murder, you have become a lawbreaker.	**Matthew 5:17-19 (see also 5:21-22, 27-28)** "Do not think that I have come to abolish the Law or the Prophets; I have not come to abolish them but to fulfill them. For truly I tell you, until heaven and earth disappear, not the smallest letter, not the least stroke of a pen, will by any means disappear from the Law until everything is accomplished. Therefore anyone who sets aside one of the least of these commands and teaches others accordingly will be called least in the kingdom of heaven, but whoever practices and teaches these commands will be called great in the kingdom of heaven."
James 2:13 Judgment without mercy will be shown to anyone who has not been merciful. Mercy triumphs over judgment.	**Matthew 5:7 and 6:14-15** "Blessed are the merciful, for they will be shown mercy." "If you forgive other people when they sin against you, your heavenly Father will also forgive you. But if you do not forgive others their sins, your Father will not forgive your sins."
James 3:12 My brothers and sisters, can a fig tree bear olives, or a grapevine bear figs? Neither can a salt spring produce fresh water.	**Matthew 7:17-18** "Likewise, every good tree bears good fruit, but a bad tree bears bad fruit. A good tree cannot bear bad fruit, and a bad tree cannot bear good fruit."
James 3:17 But the wisdom that comes from heaven is first of all pure; then peace-loving, considerate, submissive, full of mercy and good fruit, impartial and sincere.	**Matthew 5:5** "Blessed are the meek, for they will inherit the earth."
James 3:18 Peacemakers who sow in peace reap a harvest of right-eousness.	**Matthew 5:9** "Blessed are the peacemakers, for they will be called children of God."
James 4:2-3 You do not have because you do not ask God. When you ask, you do not receive, because you ask with wrong motives, that you may spend what you get on your pleasures.	**Matthew 7:7-8** "Ask and it will be given to you; seek and you will find; knock and the door will be opened to you. For everyone who asks receives; the one who seeks finds; and to the one who knocks, the door will be opened."

Comparing James and Sermon on the Mount (Continued)

LETTER OF JAMES	SERMON ON THE MOUNT
James 4:9-10 Grieve, mourn and wail. Change your laughter to mourning and your joy to gloom. Humble yourselves before the Lord, and he will lift you up.	**Matthew 5:4** "Blessed are those who mourn, for they will be comforted."
James 4:11-12 Brothers and sisters, do not slander one another. Anyone who speaks against a brother or sister or judges them speaks against the law and judges it. When you judge the law, you are not keeping it, but sitting in judgment on it. There is only one Lawgiver and Judge, the one who is able to save and destroy. But you—who are you to judge your neighbor?	**Matthew 7:1-2** "Do not judge, or you too will be judged. For in the same way you judge others, you will be judged, and with the measure you use, it will be measured to you."
James 4:14 Why, you do not even know what will happen tomorrow. What is your life? You are a mist that appears for a little while and then vanishes.	**Matthew 6:30** "If that is how God clothes the grass of the field, which is here today and tomorrow is thrown into the fire, will he not much more clothe you—you of little faith?"
James 4:15 Instead, you ought to say, "If it is the Lord's will, we will live and do this or that."	**Matthew 6:10** "Your kingdom come, your will be done, on earth as it is in heaven."
James 5:2 Your wealth has rotted, and moths have eaten your clothes.	**Matthew 6:19-21** "Do not store up for yourselves treasures on earth, where moths and vermin destroy, and where thieves break in and steal. But store up for yourselves treasures in heaven, where moths and vermin do not destroy, and where thieves do not break in and steal. For where your treasure is, there your heart will be also."
James 5:10 Brothers and sisters, as an example of patience in the face of suffering, take the prophets who spoke in the name of the Lord.	**Matthew 5:11-12** "Blessed are you when people insult you, persecute you and falsely say all kinds of evil against you because of me. Rejoice and be glad, because great is your reward in heaven, for in the same way they persecuted the prophets who were before you."
James 5:12 Above all, my brothers and sisters, do not swear—not by heaven or by earth or by anything else. All you need to say is a simple "Yes" or "No." Otherwise you will be condemned.	**Matthew 5:34-37** "But I tell you, do not swear an oath at all: either by heaven, for it is God's throne; or by the earth, for it is his footstool. . . . All you need to say is simply 'Yes' or 'No'; anything beyond this comes from the evil one."

How then can we summarize the letter of James? There are, after all, a number of handy ways people have summarized the Gospels. For example, it is said that Matthew presents Jesus as the Messiah, that Mark presents Jesus as Suffering Servant, that Luke presents Jesus as the Son of Man and that in John Jesus is the Christ, the "Son of God." If that is the case, then James presents Jesus as Teacher and Lord.

Jesus' influence is also seen in James's teaching style. While parables were not unique to Jesus in the ancient world, they certainly were prominent in his teaching. Likewise, James uses mini-parables to drive home his points. Though they are not as elaborate or perhaps as inventive as those of Jesus, they serve the purpose quite well. James uses other colorful metaphors and figures of speech to make his prose memorable and effective, as seen in the chart "Mini-Parables in James."

Commentators have offered many outlines for the book of James. It has been a notoriously difficult book to pin down because James some-times seems to proceed from point to point without clear connections. Despite the diversity among commentators about the structure of James, a synthesis or consensus of several outlines in simple form might look like this:

1. Introduction (1:1)
2. Opening Themes (1:2-27)
3. Partiality and Faith (2:1-26)
4. Words, Wisdom and Wealth (3:1–5:11)
5. Closing Exhortations (5:12-20)

This guide is based on the divisions of the *James* LifeGuide Bible Study. Since James is so dense, it is sometimes helpful to break up thought units so they can be digested more easily in one session—whether for individual study or in group discussion.

We could say more about the themes of James. But that is what the rest of this book is intended to guide you into. So, let's move ahead and see what this practical and challenging letter has to say to us.

Mini-Parables in James

James 1:10-11	The Wild Flower Scorched by the Sun
James 1:23-25	The Man Who Looks in a Mirror and Forgets What He Looks Like
James 2:2-4	The Rich Man and the Poor Man Come to Church
James 2:15-16	The Good Wishes That Don't Help Someone in Need
James 3:3	The Horse Guided by a Bit
James 3:4	The Large Ship Guided by a Small Rudder
James 3:5	The Forest Set Ablaze by a Small Fire
James 3:10-12	Springs That Only Produce Fresh or Salt Water
James 3:12	Fig Trees Don't Bear Olives
James 3:12	Grapevines Don't Produce Figs
James 4:13-15	The Merchant Who Thinks He Can Plan for Tomorrow

HOW TO USE LifeGuide® IN DEPTH

The Bible is God's Word to his people. In it and through it we find life and wisdom for life. Most importantly, the Scriptures point us to Christ, who is the culmination of God's revelation to us of who he is. The LifeGuide in Depth Bible Study series has been created for those who want to go deeply into the Bible and deeply into Christ.

Going deeply will require time and effort. But the reward will be well worth it. If your desire is a richer understanding of God's Word, if you want to grasp Scripture at a level and in dimensions you've not engaged in before, these in-depth studies are for you.

This series emphasizes

- taking passages seriously as a whole

- seeing how each passage connects to and is built on the rest of Scripture

- applying the truth of each passage to individuals and to our Christian communities

How do we do this? Each session follows a four-part format:

- **Part 1. Investigate**—Getting an overview of the passage as a whole.

- **Part 2. Connect: Scripture to Scripture**— Seeing how the passage or theme connects to other parts of the Bible.

- **Part 3. Reflect**—Pondering a key theme in the passage through a short reading.

- **Part 4. Discuss: Putting It All Together**— Tying together as a group the various themes from the first three parts and learning to apply the passage to real life.

Though groups and individuals may use LifeGuide in Depth studies in different ways and formats, the most straightforward way to use the guides is for individuals to study the first three sections on their own before each group meeting. Those first three sections are best done over several days rather than in one sitting, as individuals will typically need a total of three to four hours to work through them. Part four then offers a forty-five- to sixty-minute group discussion that guides members in putting together everything they've learned.

LifeGuide in Depth Bible Studies can be used by people of various ages, from teenagers to seniors and everyone in between. Groups can be church-related home small groups and Sunday-school classes, women's and men's Bible studies, neighborhood Bible studies, and university campus small groups. And the guides can be used on a weekly or biweekly basis, or could even form the core of a retreat weekend.

AN OVERVIEW OF THE FOUR PARTS

Part 1. Investigate (On Your Own). Inductive Bible study is at the core of LifeGuide in Depth studies. Allowing for in-depth study of one passage, an inductive approach to Scripture has three main parts: we first carefully observe what is in the text, then interpret what we are to learn from what we observe and finally apply the meaning of the passage to our own lives. This is accomplished through the use of open-ended questions that help people discover the Bible for themselves. The goal is to come to the passage with fresh eyes, not supposing we know all that it means ahead of time, but looking to see what God might have to teach us anew.

Inductive study is not meant to be mechanical; Scripture is not data that we manipulate toward a certain output. Nor does it imply that we can master Scripture. Rather we expect the Word to master us. But believing that God uses our understanding to touch our hearts and that he uses our hearts to touch our understanding, inductive study can help us draw near to God. It's a tool to guide our hearts and minds toward Christ through his Word. For more on inductive study we recommend *Transforming Bible Study* by Bob Grahmann and *The Bible Study Handbook* by Lindsay Olesberg.

Part one of each session is a revised edition of the original LifeGuide Bible study guide. LifeGuide Bible studies have been the leading series for individuals and groups studying Scripture for almost thirty years. They have given millions of people a solid grasp of the Bible. The LifeGuide in Depth Bible Study series, like the original LifeGuides, honors the context of each book of the Bible and the original message of each biblical author, and guides readers into application of God's Word. Relevant excerpts from *The IVP Bible Background Commentary: New Testament* and *The IVP Bible Background Commentary: Old Testament* have been added to these studies to offer helpful historical and cultural information about each passage. These excerpts appear as callouts in part one of each guide.

Part 2. Connect: Scripture to Scripture (On Your Own). One of the most important ways of understanding any particular passage of Scripture is to uncover how it stands in the pathway of the rest of Scripture. The historical, cultural and literary background of any passage is critical, and how biblical writers draw on previous Scripture offers a wealth of meaning to readers. The purpose of part two of each session is to draw this out.

The original writers and readers of the books of the Bible were thoroughly immersed in the Scripture written beforehand. It was the air they breathed. So when they wrote, earlier Scripture passages and themes were an inseparable part of how they thought and taught. Thus, understanding the New Testament often requires knowing the Old Testament allusions, themes or direct quotations found there. And usually it is not enough to know the one particular Old Testament verse being quoted or referenced. We need to understand the context of that verse in the chapter and book in which it is found. Neglecting this can lead readers astray in their interpretations or applications.

For example, in Mark 6:47-50, Jesus walks on the lake during a storm and is "about to pass by [the disciples]" (v. 48), who are struggling for survival in a boat. Does Jesus not see them? Doesn't he care they are in danger? Why does he intend to "pass by"? What's going on? The answer is found by going back to the Old Testament. In Exodus 33:19–34:7 and 1 Kings 19:10-11, God "passes by" Moses and Elijah to reveal himself in a clear and dramatic way. Mark uses the same phrase (which his readers would recognize) to indicate that Jesus is making a similar dramatic revelation of divine character.

In making these connections, it is usually more helpful to go backward than to go forward. That is, we should first investigate Scripture written before the passage being studied was written. For instance, in seeking to understand the Psalms, we should first go to the earlier books of the Old Testament rather than to the New Testament. The psalmists knew and perhaps had memorized large portions of Genesis, Exodus and so forth. That was the raw material they were working with; those were their sources. If we don't understand how and why they built on these, we won't understand fully what they are saying.

Take the "suffering servant" of Isaiah 52–53. Although New Testament writers linked Jesus to the suffering servant, we shouldn't "read back" into Isaiah the notion that the servant was a divine figure. The text in Isaiah does not indicate that and we would be misreading the text to insist that it does. Nonetheless, it is entirely appropriate to use this image, as Jesus did, to gain a greater understanding of another dimension of who Jesus was and what he came to do.

In part two, then, we will mostly, but not exclusively, go back to Scripture that predates the passage we are studying for better understanding.

Part 3. Reflect (On Your Own). In part three you will find a reading that expands on one of the themes of the study. It may contain a story or commentary on the passage, or both. And it may be drawn from some other Christian author or source, whether contemporary or ancient. In any case, it is intended to help focus your mind in a single direction after the wide variety of issues raised in parts one and two. A couple of questions at the end of the reading will help you crystallize what you have learned.

Part 4. Discuss: Putting It All Together (With a Group). This part is, as the name describes, intended for group discussion. You can work through it on your own too, but some questions are repetitive with questions from the first three parts. This is intentional and necessary for group discussion; after individuals in a group have worked through each passage on their own during the week, they will want to hear from each other what they have learned and thought about. If you decide you do want to go through part four by yourself anyway, you can skip those questions that were found earlier or use those questions as opportunities to think again about key ideas. Reviewing the content is a good way for groups *and* individuals to lock those ideas into their hearts and minds.

Groups should begin the discussion with the "Open" question and then read the passage together. Everyone will have been over the passage several times already, but reading aloud in a group can actually bring new insight.

Below are a few suggestions for group members that can facilitate rich discussion and insight:

1. Come to the study prepared. Follow the suggestions for individual study mentioned above. You will find that careful preparation will greatly enrich your time spent in group discussion.

2. Be willing to participate in the discussion. The leader of your group will not be lecturing. Instead, she or he will be asking the questions found in this guide and encouraging the members of the group to discuss what they have learned.

3. Stick to the topic being discussed. These studies focus on a particular passage of Scripture. This allows everyone to participate on equal ground and fosters in-depth study.

4. Be sensitive to the other members of the group. Listen attentively when they describe what they have learned. You may be surprised by their insights! Also note that each question assumes a variety of answers; many questions do not have "right" answers, particularly questions that aim at meaning or application. Instead the questions push us to explore the passage more thoroughly.

   When possible, link what you say to the comments of others. Also, be affirming whenever you can. This will encourage some of the more hesitant members of the group to participate.

5. Be careful not to dominate the discussion. We are sometimes so eager to express our thoughts that we leave too little opportunity for others to respond. By all means participate! But allow others to do so also.

6. Expect God to teach you through the passage being discussed and through the other members of the group. Pray that you will have an enjoyable and profitable time together, but also that as a result of the study you will find ways to take action individually and/or as a group.

7. It will be helpful for groups to follow a few basic guidelines. These guidelines, which you may wish to adapt to your situation, should be read at the beginning of the first session.

   • Anything said in the group is considered confidential and will not be discussed outside the group unless specific permission is given to do so.

   • We will provide time for each person present to talk if he or she feels comfortable doing so.

- We will talk about ourselves and our own situations, avoiding conversation about other people.
- We will listen attentively to each other.
- We will be very cautious about giving advice.

Additional suggestions for the group leader can be found at the back of the guide.

Plunging into the depths of God's wisdom and love is a glorious adventure. Like Paul said in 1 Corinthians 2:9-10: "As it is written: 'What no eye has seen, what no ear has heard, and what no human mind has conceived'—the things God has prepared for those who love him—these are the things God has revealed to us by his Spirit. The Spirit searches all things, even the deep things of God." As you go in depth into Scripture, may the Spirit reveal the deep things of God's own self to you.

DEPENDABLE OR DOUBLE-MINDED?

James 1:1-18

WHERE WE'RE GOING*

Sometimes people have the mistaken impression that just because they follow God and do what he says, everything in life should turn out great. No more problems, difficulties or disappointments. That's what those who first read James's letter two thousand years ago thought too. Why does life often seem so hard even after we commit ourselves to Jesus? That's where James begins his letter, so that's where we'll begin too. We'll dig deeply into the first part of James 1 in four sections.

Part 1.   Investigate: James 1:1-18 (On Your Own)

Part 2.   Connect: Scripture to Scripture (On Your Own)

Part 3.   Reflect: The Process of Character (On Your Own)

Part 4.   Discuss: Putting It All Together (With a Group)

A PRAYER TO PRAY

Here's a prayer you can use to set you on your way:

Father, Son and Spirit, gracious triune God of love, we know that every good and perfect gift comes to us from you. You shine light in darkness, and remain steady and constant in a world that is always changing. You generously provide all we need when we face difficult times. So we ask you to open our eyes to see your Word of truth as we begin our study of James. Give us the wisdom we need so that we will remain steadfast when trials come and so that our very lives might become a gift we give back to you in gratitude. Amen.

---

*Though these studies can be used in a variety of ways and formats, for maximum benefit we recommend doing parts one, two and three on your own and then working through the questions in part four with a group.

PART 1. INVESTIGATE
James 1:1-18
(On Your Own)

Read James 1:1-18.

1:1. *Josephus and some later Jewish-Christian writers reported the great esteem that fellow Jerusalemites, especially the poor, had for James. Non-Christian as well as Christian Jerusalemites admired his piety, but his denunciations of the aristocracy (as in 5:1-6) undoubtedly played a large role in the aristocratic priesthood's opposition to him. About the year A.D. 62, . . . the high priest Ananus II executed James and some other people. The public outcry was so great, however, that . . . Ananus was deposed from the high priesthood over the matter.*

1. What are the different situations described in James 1:1-18 in which Christians need to persevere?

   testing, trials, lack wisdom "lowly", trial

2. How do you respond to the idea that we should "consider it pure joy" whenever we "face trials of many kinds" (v. 2)?

   it doesn't sound possible

3. How are perseverance and maturity developed in us by enduring trials (vv. 3-4)?

   because it produces endurance, and endurance makes us complete

4. What difficult experiences have increased your perseverance and maturity?

   difficulties at work and relationally

1:5. *The prime Old Testament example of asking God (cf. 4:2-3) for wisdom is 1 Kings 3:5 and 9 (cf. also in the Apocrypha, Wisdom of Solomon 8:21; 9:5; Ecclus 51:13-14), and God was always recognized as its source (e.g., Prov 2:6). In Jewish wisdom, upbraiding or reproaching was considered harsh and rude under normal circumstances, although reproof was honorable.*

5. How might trials expose our need for God's wisdom (v. 5)?

   because we won't know how to endure

6. Under pressure, how does the faithful Christian (vv. 5-6) contrast with the person described in verses 6-8?

   Knowing God will always provide you with wisdom vs not and being tossed by anything that comes your way

7. In the context of trials and perseverance, why does James contrast rich and poor Christians (vv. 9-11)?

   because the poor persevere while the rich will fade away

8. In what ways do you tend to rely on your possessions?

all sorts of ways. I think stuff will bring me joy and peace and security

9. How are temptations different from trials (vv. 2–16)?

trials happen to us. temptations are based on our desires as a human

10. What role does God play when we face trials and when we face temptations (vv. 2–16)?

God can be there through trials, provide wisdom, helps us endure
God does not tempt us

11. How is God the ultimate example of goodness and dependability (vv. 16–18)?

he is steadfast. good things come from him

How is this truth a source of joy and hope for you?

12. Think of trials or temptations you are currently facing. How can this passage encourage you to depend on God?

He is good throughout my questioning

Talk to God about your trials and temptations and your need for his wisdom in those situations. Ask him to help you to learn to persevere and to be like him in his goodness and dependability.

1:13-16. *In most Jewish texts, Satan (also called Belial and Mastema) fills the role of tempter. Although James does not deny Satan's indirect role (4:7), he emphasizes here the human element in succumbing to temptation. . . . The meaning [of "test"] is [likely] as in Ecclesiasticus 15:11-12 and 20 [from the Apocrypha]: people choose to sin, and they dare not say that God is responsible for their response to testing (by contrast, Greek literature was full of people protesting that their temptation was too great to resist).*

PART 2. CONNECT
Scripture to Scripture
(On Your Own)

THE TWELVE TRIBES

Who are "the twelve tribes scattered among the nations" that James directs his letter to (v. 1)? The nation of Israel began with a single man—Abraham, who lived perhaps four thousand years ago. Originally called Abram, he was born in Ur of the Chaldees in modern-day southeastern Iraq.

In Genesis 12:1-9 God tells him to go with his whole household to Canaan on the eastern coast of the Mediterranean Sea. In doing so, God promises Abraham several things. Read Genesis 12:1-3 and list the different promises:

> make you a great nation
> bless you. you will be a blessing
> make you famous
> bless/curse those who bless/curse you
> all families will be blessed through you

God gave a son, Isaac, to Abraham and his wife, Sarah. In turn, Isaac—to whom God gave the name *Israel*—had a son named Jacob, who had twelve sons of his own (see Genesis 35:23-26). Each of these sons became the patriarch of a tribe. All of the tribes increased during the four hundred years that they were in Egypt. Thus, even during their years of oppression and enslavement in Egypt, God's promise to Abraham was fulfilled.

After Moses led Israel out of Egypt, God gave the nation the Ten Commandments and other instructions on how they were to live. He also (through Moses) gave them a promise and a warning regarding the Promised Land that he was leading them to possess as their own.

Paraphrase the warning found in Deuteronomy 4:25-27.

> do not worship anything else, if you break my
> covenant you will be scattered/destroyed

In contrast, what promise is offered in Deuteronomy 4:40?

> if you obey, all will be well

Because the nation disobeyed God, the tribes and people of Israel were scattered. The prophet Amos brought God's word against them for the twin sins of worshiping other gods and oppressing the poor. After the northern tribes of Israel rejected God's ways, they were conquered by Assyria as is summarized in 1 Kings 17. This left only the tribe of Judah in the land and some of the small tribe of Benjamin. So, long before the time of James, the tribes of Israel were scattered, expelled from Palestine.

Yet God in his mercy promised that one day, at the end of the age when the Messiah comes, all the scattered tribes of Israel will be regathered. Isaiah 11:1-10 describes what this will be like: "The wolf will live with the lamb, the leopard will lie down with the goat, the calf and the lion and the yearling together; and a little child will lead them" (v. 6). Isaiah continues:

> In that day the Lord will reach out his hand a second time to reclaim the surviving remnant of his people from Assyria, from Lower Egypt, from Upper Egypt, from Cush, from Elam, from Babylonia, from Hamath and from the islands of the Mediterranean.
>
> He will raise a banner for the nations
>   and gather the exiles of Israel;
> he will assemble the scattered people of Judah
>   from the four corners of the earth. (Isaiah 11:11-12)

We find a similar prophecy in Jeremiah 31:8-14 and Zechariah 8:7-8 and 10:6-12. Craig Keener writes, "Most Jewish people believed that ten of the twelve tribes had been lost for centuries, and they would be restored only at the end of the age."[1] Then Israel would worship one God instead of committing idolatry and would be just to the poor instead of oppressing them.

Only the tribes of Judah and Benjamin remained in Palestine in Jesus' day. By addressing his letter "to the twelve tribes," James is suggesting that all twelve tribes have been found among those who believe Jesus is Lord. Jesus has ushered in the final age—but the kingdom has not fully come. The kingdom is already here in some respects, but not yet completely. James acknowledges that the twelve tribes have been identified, as the prophets said that they would in the age to come. But he also says they are scattered, as Jesus' followers had been scattered across the Mediterranean basin by persecution. The kingdom has dawned, but much that is imperfect remains.

Likewise for us, while trials and temptations remain for the moment, we hold firm to the hope of Jesus' final triumph while we wait.

Read Matthew 19:28-29. What does Jesus say about the final age?

people who have followed will sit on 12 thrones
12 tribes back together

COUNT IT ALL JOY

As we noted in the introduction to James (see the chart comparing James and the Sermon on the Mount), we will see throughout James's letter that he often seems to offer a commentary on Jesus' sermon (Matthew 5–7). Here is one of the first instances in which we see how they interconnect.

What similarities do you see between James 1:2, 12 and Matthew 5:11-12?

have a positive reaction to hardship, and those who are rewarded tend to be opposite

In fact, all of James 1:1-18 can be seen as an expansion on these two verses in Matthew. James includes Jesus' particular focus—persecution because of our loyalty to Jesus—but is addressing a wider range of "trials of many kinds" that are not included in the passage in Matthew. He also offers an extended explanation of why such trials would be a cause for rejoicing.

ASKING GOD FOR WISDOM

James also has a fair amount to say about wisdom. In verse 5, he emphasizes the importance of asking God for wisdom.

The book of the Bible best known for the theme of wisdom is Proverbs. But wisdom is emphasized throughout the rest of the Old Testament as well. Wisdom in the Bible is not just being smart, intelligent or educated, though it does not exclude those. Rather, first, biblical wisdom is defined as "skill for living."[2]

One of the early mentions of wisdom is found in Exodus 28:3 and 31:2-5. According to these verses, what does wisdom give people the ability to do?

mastering things, but knowing how to do things specifically from God

Second, wisdom is also _evident when people obey God's law._ For example, Deuteronomy 4:5-6 says,

See, I have taught you decrees and laws as the LORD my God commanded me, so that you may follow them in the land you are entering to take possession of it. Observe them carefully, for this will show your wisdom and understanding to the nations, who will hear about all these decrees and say, "Surely this great nation is a wise and understanding people." (See also Deuteronomy 34:9 and Proverbs 4:4-5 among many passages.)

The foolish ignore God's words and his commands. The wise hold them close.

Third, Scripture reveals that wisdom is _especially important for rulers._ As Solomon asked God, "Give me wisdom and knowledge, that I may lead this people, for who is able to govern this great people of yours?" (2 Chronicles 1:10; see also Ezra 7:25).

What does governing with wisdom look like in particular? In 1 Kings 3:16-28 we read the famous story of Solomon trying to determine which of two women is the real mother of a baby. So he gives the order to divide the child and give half to each. The one who wanted the child to live was the true parent. The one who was willing for the child to die was not.

In 1 Kings 3:28, it says Israel was in awe when they heard this story because Solomon had the wisdom to do what?

for rendering justice, Knowing how to learn who was the real mother

We find this same theme in Psalm 37:30. The verse is an example of parallelism—a common poetic form in which the same idea is repeated for emphasis in two different ways. What does the psalmist say speaking wisdom is equivalent to?

walking on a path - not straying
Knowing right from wrong

Proverbs 2:9-10 also tells us that wisdom is equivalent to doing what is just and right. How do Jeremiah 7:5-6 and 22:3 define what it means to do what is just and right?

being merciful to everyone, caring for the oppressed

The Old Testament tells us that one of the key ways wisdom is shown is by doing justice for the poor, the oppressed. To execute this kind of justice is a matter for individuals to be concerned about, but it especially pertains to how rulers and nations show wisdom.

In fact, Isaiah 11:1-5, which we looked at earlier, makes this very point about wisdom when it describes how the Messiah will rule in the age to come. First, Isaiah 11:2 describes four ways in which the Spirit will rest on him. Fill in what's missing.

The Spirit of _the Lord_ will rest upon him—
    the Spirit of _wisdom_ and _understanding_,
    the Spirit of _counsel_ and _might_,
    the Spirit of _Knowledge_ and _fear of the Lord._

Then Isaiah 11:3-4 describes how he will use this wisdom to judge—with righteousness for the poor and justice for the needy. Rulers and governors of nations show wisdom when they help those who are oppressed, who do not have power in society, rather than side with the rich and powerful.

This is one of the main kinds of wisdom James has in mind as we will see throughout his letter. Where do you see this kind of wisdom under consideration in James 1:1-18?

v9 - lowly raised high, rich humbled

Blessed Is the Man

James alludes to the Psalms when he offers a description in verse 12 of the kind of person who is blessed. In fact the whole book of Psalms begins with this famous phrase: "Blessed is the man who walks not in the counsel of the wicked, nor stands in the way of sinners, nor sits in the seat of scoffers" (ESV). Read Psalm 1.

How is this description of someone who meditates on God's Word and is rooted like a tree (rather than easily blown by the wind) similar to the description found in James 1:5-8?

those who doubt God's ability to give wisdom
are blown by the wind. trials will blow them
around

James likely expects his readers to recognize this reference to Psalm 1 and bring all of its riches and meaning to mind as they read his letter.

How can God's Word become a source of stability in your life?

we can gain wisdom from it, and use it to
bring steadfastness in our lives

Testing and Temptation

James also offers a brief primer on temptation in this first chapter of his letter. He tells us that God tests, but he does not tempt. The purpose of a test or trial is to reveal what is inside (the character of a person). The point of temptation is to cause someone to fail. When Moses led the people of Israel out of slavery in Egypt to the desert (Deuteronomy 8:2; 13:1-5) it was not God's purpose for them to fail. Rather, God's purpose was for good. As James says in 1:12-18, God doesn't give temptations. He gives good gifts instead. Sin brings death (1:15). God's gifts on the other hand bring us forth, giving birth to new life in us by his word of truth (1:18).

What was the purpose of various trials God sent Israel according to Amos 4:10-11?

to have His people return to Him

We must be careful not to lightly brush away the pain and sorrow that comes with suffering and trials, as if to say they don't really matter. They do matter and they mark us deeply. At the same time, when we are able to look back, we can see that God's hand was in our lives during those troubled times, and that he helped us grow in character, in strength and in our closeness to him.

Even more than that, James says the early Christians were a kind of "firstfruits of all he created" (1:18). The firstfruits were offerings called for in the Old Testament (see Deuteronomy 18:3-5; 26:1-10; Numbers 18:8-12). These sacrifices of just a part of a harvest symbolized that the whole harvest belonged to God. Likewise, for James, the early Christians symbolized a much larger harvest of all God's people who were to be made alive by his Word. That is indeed cause for joy.

[1]Craig Keener, _The IVP Bible Background Commentary: New Testament_ (Downers Grove, IL: InterVarsity Press, 1993), p. 690.
[2]Leland Ryken, James C. Wilhoit and Tremper Longman III, eds., _Dictionary of Biblical Imagery_ (Downers Grove, IL: InterVarsity Press, 1998), p. 955.

PART 3. REFLECT
The Process of Character
(On Your Own)

The musical based on Victor Hugo's novel *Les Misérables* begins in France in the early 1800s. An ex-con, Jean Valjean, is on his way to see his probation officer after nineteen years on a chain gang. He stops at the house of a bishop, where he is welcomed warmly with a hot meal and a night's stay; Valjean repays this kindness by stealing the bishop's silverware. The next day he is captured by the police and returned to the bishop for confirmation of his thievery.

Yes, the bishop confirms, this man stayed with him the previous night. Then the bishop turns to Valjean and asks why he didn't take the candlesticks too. They could have been sold for two hundred francs. He should have taken them along with the flatware.

The police are shocked. What Valjean told them was true? He hadn't stolen the silver? It had been given to him, an ex-con, by the bishop? They can hardly believe it. But the bishop insists and sends the police on their way without the thief.

Before Valjean leaves, however, the bishop tells him, "Jean Valjean, my brother, you no longer belong to evil but to good. It is your soul I am buying for you. I withdraw it from dark thoughts and from the spirit of perdition, and I give it to God!"[1] As a result, Valjean's life is radically transformed, and we see him sacrificing dramatically for others through the rest of the story.

The over sixty million people worldwide who have seen and heard the musical based on Hugo's novel are just as astonished as the police at the bishop's amazing act of grace. In the face of being clearly wronged, the bishop does not call for punishment but literally redeems Valjean, buying him back from imprisonment and darkness and setting him free for a new life. We wonder if we could ever have done such a thing. How could the bishop have suddenly had this stroke of wisdom, courage and strength to give and forgive so generously?

The answer is that this was not a spontaneous act of mercy. It was behavior shaped and honed over years. This encounter between the bishop and Valjean is where the musical begins, but it is not where the novel begins.

In the novel we learn that years before, the bishop had opened his spacious residence to the patients from the overcrowded hospital next door, while he himself moved into the tiny hospital. He walked to make pastoral visits so he could distribute his own carriage allowance to poor mothers, widows and orphans. When a subordinate refused to visit a murderer on death row, the bishop did not rebuke the subordinate but went to the murderer and showed him how to be reconciled with God. He even convinced a gang of thieves he once encountered to make contributions to the poor.

For over fifty dense pages Hugo chronicles dozens of similar episodes in the bishop's life before he ever meets Valjean. The dramatic act did not emerge from nowhere but emerged out of a lifelong pattern.

This is the very point James seeks to make in his New Testament letter. Character does not result from a single dramatic act of wisdom, and grace is not fully constructed overnight. Rather, they are built, brick by brick and board by board, throughout a life.[2] James spells out the process clearly in 1:3-4:

TESTING → PERSEVERANCE → MATURITY

While God's grace may come to us in sudden bursts of light and life, our character is built to maturity and completeness over time and through many difficulties. In 1:12 James adds one further stage in this process, the final result of persevering under trial: the crown of life. And so we have:

TESTING → PERSEVERANCE →
MATURITY → CROWN OF LIFE

Likewise, selfish, unforgiving, angry or foolish character does not become full blown in us in one day. Rather, James says that this kind of character too is the result of a steady stream of decisions and actions in the face of trials. He lays it out like this in 1:14-15:

EVIL DESIRE → TEMPTATION → SIN →
DEATH

Comparing the pattern of evil and sin to the life cycle, James explains that evil desire is first conceived, which then gives birth to sin and ultimately ends in death. Notice how this four-stage process parallels and contrasts with the four stages of a mature and complete character. One ends in the crown of life. The other in death.

Because character development is a process that can last years or a whole life, one act of grace is not the end of the road. Neither, however, is one failure. The course of our character is not destined by a single episode. We can change course. For good or for ill, character is built, small step by small step.

When we tell the truth on a minor matter rather than slant it in our favor, when we support community efforts to help those without financial resources, when we pray to God in trust that he will get us through a crisis—each of these steps, consistently practiced, leads to mature character. And this type of character is not one "blown and tossed by the wind" but one that is stable and unchanging like that of God our Father (1:6, 17). It is character that does not hoard wealth that is temporary but instead gives generously, as God does, without finding fault with others for being weak or lazy (1:5, 11). It is character that will lead not to death but to a crown of life (1:12, 15)—just as was the case with the good bishop in *Les Misérables*.

What's the main idea in this section?

character is built over time

What is one thing you can act on based on this reading?

not complain

---

[1]Victor Hugo, *Les Misérables* (New York: Signet, 1987), p. 106.
[2]George Stulac sees a similar progression for godly and sinful character in his *James*, InterVarsity Press New Testament Commentary (Downers Grove, IL: InterVarsity Press, 1993), pp. 35-39, 52-55.

PART 4. DISCUSS
Putting It All Together
(With a Group)

OPEN

Think about when you have been in great shape physically. How does this compare and contrast to being in good shape spiritually?

READ JAMES 1:1-18.

No pain. No gain. Or so the saying goes. Athletes remind themselves of this to get their best possible performance. Sometimes they have to go through grueling training. Without it, there is no improvement. James suggests it is the same for Christians.

1. What is significant about the fact that James is writing to "the twelve tribes scattered among the nations" (v. 1)?

2. How are temptations different from trials (vv. 2-16)?

3. Typically we think of being wise as being intelligent, shrewd or insightful. That's not the emphasis found in the Old Testament, however. What did you learn about the Old Testament understanding of wisdom from part two, "Connect: Scripture to Scripture"?

4. In your own life, where do you need the three kinds of wisdom discussed in "Connect: Scripture to Scripture"?

5. Martin Luther, when speaking of temptation, famously said, "You can't stop the birds from flying over your head, but you can stop them from nesting in your hair." James also makes a distinction between evil desire and sin. The first leads to the second, but the two are not the same. Think about the evil desires and sins you wrestle with. How would you explain the difference between the two?

6. When you have been tempted by a desire to gossip or shade the truth or lust or get angry, what have you found helpful in keeping that desire from giving birth to sin?

7. The reading for part three, "Reflect: The Process of Character," says that developing character is a process, that maturity doesn't come all at once. Do you agree? Why or why not?

8. What good habits have you seen shape your character or the character of others?

9. As was said in part three, God wants character that is not "blown and tossed by the wind" but one that is stable and unchanging like that of God our Father (1:6, 17). How can we develop a more stable faith, the kind James describes?

10. It can seem strange that we should consider trials and tests a cause for joy. After working through this first part of James, how might you begin to explain why we can, in fact, see trials with joy?

11. One of the best ways to appreciate God's dependability is to recall the different ways he has shown his faithfulness in the past. How have you seen God's reliability—his "good and perfect gifts," his unchanging character—at work?

Take time to thank and praise God for his steadfastness.

WORDS, WORDS, WORDS

James 1:19-27

WHERE WE'RE GOING

In the first part of chapter 1, James begins to unpack the biblical notion of wisdom. It's much more than being smart or clever. It means living the way God desires us to live, following his instructions so that our character becomes consistent and steadfast in the face of difficulties that come along.

Trials, in particular, provide an opportunity to gain wisdom. Some people do just that when life goes wrong—they grow in strength and love. Others, however, become cynical and hardhearted. What makes the difference? In this last part of chapter 1, James begins to answer this critical question.

Part 1. Investigate: James 1:19-27 (On Your Own)

Part 2. Connect: Scripture to Scripture (On Your Own)

Part 3. Reflect: Words to Live By (On Your Own)

Part 4. Discuss: Putting It All Together (With a Group)

A PRAYER TO PRAY

God, our Father, you are the source of all that is right and good in the world. From you comes the power to save, to bring us back into right relationship with you. For this we give you great thanks and praise. We ask that you will, by your presence and power in us, give us the strength to be quick to listen to your Word, slow to speak your Word and slow to become angry in your name. We ask this so that we may give ourselves in love to the weak and poor who do not have this world's power, and yet not come under the influence of this world's power ourselves. Amen.

PART 1. INVESTIGATE
James 1:19-27

Read James 1:19-27.

1. What do you learn about what God desires from us?

    he desires us to be doers of the word. to help those in need and not succumb to the world

2. Look back at James 1:18 and then again at 1:19-27. Given the context of 1:18, what kind of listening does James want his readers to be quick to practice?

3. How can being quick to listen and slow to speak help us be slow to become angry (v. 19)?

4. When have you seen or experienced the truth that "human anger does not produce the righteousness that God desires" (v. 20)?

    1:20. *The militant Jewish resistance emphasized striking out at the Romans and their aristocratic vassals, supposing that they [the militants] would be acting as agents of God's righteous indignation. But James associates righteousness with peace (3:18) and nonresistance (5:7).*

5. James tells us that God's Word was planted in us. What weeds can choke that Word and keep it from growing (v. 21)? Explain.

6. In your own words explain how the person who merely listens is different from the one who puts God's Word into practice (vv. 22-25).

1:23-24. *The best mirrors were of Corinthian bronze, but no mirrors of that period produced the accurate images available today (cf. 1 Cor 13:12). Those with enough resources to own mirrors used them when fixing their hair; if James alludes to such people, he portrays the forgetful hearer as stupid. More likely, he refers to many people who had no mirrors and saw themselves rarely, who might more naturally forget their own appearance. In this case the reference is to the ease with which one loses the memory of the word, if one does not work hard to put it into practice.*

1:27. *In contrast to the violent and unruly religion of the Jewish revolutionaries, true religion involves defending the socially powerless (Ex 22:20-24; Ps 146:9; Is 1:17) and avoiding worldliness (i.e., the values and behavior of the world). . . . Orphans and widows had neither direct means of support nor automatic legal defenders in that society.*

7. Why is there a tendency for Christians to listen to and yet not follow God's Word?

8. How can you avoid this tendency?

9. According to verses 26 and 27, how do people who think they are religious differ from those who are truly religious?

10. Based on what you've read in this chapter, do you think James would be satisfied with good works apart from our listening to and receiving God's Word? Explain.

11. Give some specific examples of how your religion could become more "pure and faultless" in the sense James has in mind in verse 27.

Ask God to help you become a better listener and doer of his Word.

PART 2. CONNECT
Scripture to Scripture

In James 1:19 we find a virtual table of contents for the rest of the book. James will take up each of the three commands in the verse later on. Robert Wall suggests[1] that besides the introduction and conclusion, the heart of James's letter can be viewed this way:

The Wisdom of "Quick to Hear"	James 1:22–2:26
The Wisdom of "Slow to Speak"	James 3:1-18
The Wisdom of "Slow to Anger"	James 4:1–5:6

Here we'll take a first look at where James drew these themes from both in the Old Testament and in the teachings of Jesus.

BE QUICK TO HEAR

When James tells us in 1:19 to be quick to hear and slow to speak, he's not just suggesting that we make sure we are polite and don't interrupt other people. He is recalling the whole Old Testament motif of what it means to hear God's Word. This becomes clear in 1:22 when he clarifies, "Do not merely listen to the word, and so deceive yourselves. Do what it says."

In James's view, we are not merely to make sure we listen to the Bible being read in church or to recordings of Scripture, as if that magically has some effect on us in itself. No, in the Bible, listening means more than allowing sound waves to bounce off our eardrums.

According to Psalms 1:1-3 and 19:7-10, how are people transformed when they internalize God's Word in a deep way?

_____

_____

_____

_____

As mentioned previously, parallelism is a common technique writers of the Old Testament used to convey their ideas. Essentially, an idea is repeated in a slightly different way to help explain and expand what is meant. Look at Deuteronomy 4:1-2. What is equivalent to hearing the decrees and laws Moses is teaching?

_____

_____

_____

_____

_____

In Deuteronomy 6:4-6 we find what is called the Shema—the centerpiece of the life and thought of Israel that was to be repeated in morning and evening prayers. Again, noting the parallelism here, what is equivalent to hearing that "The LORD our God, the LORD is one"?

_____

_____

_____

_____

The prophets often had very particular ideas about what listening should look like and what not listening all too frequently looks like. What do the following verses say *not* hearing looks like or involves?

Ezekiel 12:1-2:

_____

_____

Zechariah 7:8-14:

_____

_____

On the other hand, what does Jeremiah 21:11-12 say hearing means?

_____

_____

In James 1:1-18, we saw that wisdom was equivalent to obedience—in particular, obedience that involved doing justice. This theme is continued in the last part of James 1, but this time *hearing* is used as an image to convey obedience in general and obedience that involves doing justice in particular.

We also noted in studying James 1:1-18 that we will see James pick up many themes from Jesus' Sermon on the Mount. This is another case of that. How does Jesus describe the relationship between hearing and doing in the conclusion to the Sermon on the Mount in Matthew 7:24-27?

_____

_____

_____

_____

BE SLOW TO SPEAK

James's admonition in 1:19 to be slow to speak is certainly the flip side of being quick to listen. If we are taking care to listen carefully to others and to God, we will by definition be saying very little. Much more than this, however, is in view in the Old Testament world, where what a person said was deeply tied to who they were. Our speech reveals our inner being, whether positive or negative.

Draw lines connecting each passage to the particular aspect of our inner world revealed by words or mouths. We've done the first one for you.

Psalm 5:9   arrogance

Psalm 19:14   forgiveness of sin

Psalm 31:18   thoughts of the heart

Psalm 40:3   malice and lies

Isaiah 6:5   sin

Isaiah 6:6-7   praise

Because our character and inner being are revealed by our mouths, and because that inner world is often corrupt and sinful, the Bible cautions us to be very careful about what we say. Read the following passages and note the positive results of being slow to speak and the negative results of being quick to speak: Psalm 120:3-4, Proverbs 10:18-21, 13:3, 18:6-7 and Ecclesiastes 10:12-14.

Positive Results of Being Slow to Speak	Negative Results of Being Quick to Speak

In the world of the Old Testament, covenants, contracts and other commitments were often bound verbally, sometimes with oaths, so caution was especially called for regarding what a person said. How does Jesus echo this theme in the Sermon on the Mount in Matthew 5:33-36?

_____

_____

_____

BE SLOW TO ANGER

Just as being quick to listen is tied closely to being slow to speak, so being slow to speak is tightly connected to being slow to anger. What do each of these Proverbs say about quick words and quick anger or slow words and slow anger?

Proverbs 14:29:

_____

_____

Proverbs 15:18:

_____

_____

Proverbs 17:27:

_____

_____

Proverbs 29:20:

_____

_____

The topic of anger, like other topics James has discussed so far, is also addressed by Jesus in the Sermon on the Mount. In Matthew 5:21-22, how does Jesus express the seriousness with which he takes the issue of anger?

_____

_____

_____

_____

How does Jesus characterize the opposite of anger in Matthew 5:38-44?

_____

_____

_____

_____

_____

But what about righteous anger? you might be asking. The world is full of injustice. And Jesus himself seemed to show such a response when he overturned the moneychangers in the temple. Shouldn't we also show this kind of reaction when we see and hear about child abuse, corrupt government officials, and women and children being enslaved in sex trafficking? As we know from James 1:27, he particularly thinks at-risk women and children need our special concern.

No doubt there are times for that. But even in such cases, James is counseling us to have a slow, deliberate, thoughtful approach. Not a quick, angry, reactive response.

David Nystrom suggests it is possible "that James is instructing us to be slow to assume the mantle of righteous indignation, because in so doing we implicitly claim to speak for God."[2] This is a special word to Christian preachers, teachers and leaders who have particular responsibilities in this realm. So while James says be "slow to anger" rather than "never be angry," it is clear that a quick, unreflective, unprayerful anger is clearly outside of God's will for us, regardless of the cause.

PUT AWAY ALL FILTHINESS

James tells us in 1:21 to put away all filthiness and wickedness. This image is drawn from Zechariah 3 which tells the story of Joshua, the high priest at the time. This is not the same Joshua who led Israel into the Promised Land after Moses died. Rather this takes place hundreds of years later when the temple is being rebuilt after the exile to Babylon. Zechariah records a vision he has of the high priest in filthy garments.

Read Zechariah 3. Here Joshua is a symbol of the whole nation. What do his dirty clothes and his clean clothes each represent?

_____

_____

_____

_____

_____

_____

Why would James bring up this image and the issue of confessing sins in the context of the three themes we've looked at: being quick to hear, slow to speak and slow to become angry?

_____

_____

_____

_____

_____

_____

When James writes in 1:21, "humbly accept the word planted in you, which can save you," he doesn't mean that the Bible has some kind of magical power that can be recited like an incantation and so save us. No, it is God's Word empowered by his Spirit who lives within us that has this power. We are not to listen merely to words spoken but to our God who speaks in and through those words "to cleanse us of our sin." By "the word planted in you," James emphasizes that it is God, powerfully at work in us, who brings salvation. His word has priority. Not our words.

LOOKING IN A MIRROR AND FORGETTING

In James's story of the mirror in 1:23, looking in a mirror and forgetting what we look like is similar to hearing the Word and not doing it. It's giving "lip service" to the importance of God's Word but not taking it seriously in how we live our lives.

Once again James is drawing on a theme from the Sermon on the Mount. Look at Matthew 7:21-23. What are examples of what it would look like today to not take God's Word seriously, to say "Lord, Lord" but not obey God's will?

_____

_____

_____

_____

BRIDLE THE TONGUE

James can seem extreme in 1:26 when he says bridling the tongue is an indication of whether or not someone is religious. How does Psalm 34:12-13 express the quite pervasive influence controlling words can have on our life?

_____

_____

_____

_____

Now look at Psalm 141:3-4. How, according to the psalmist, does watching our words influence our lives?

_____

_____

_____

_____

Sometimes, having one area of our lives disciplined means that, without as much conscious effort, other aspects of our lives also become disciplined. If a student is disciplined in her studies, she will likely also carefully schedule her other responsibilities in life. If someone is focused on getting enough exercise, then eating in a careful and disciplined way seems much easier and more natural. James sees being careful about what we say as a doorway into a life that is fully committed to God.

What discipline in your life could (or does) have the effect of helping you be disciplined in other areas as well? Explain.

_____

_____

_____

_____

WIDOWS AND ORPHANS

James says in 1:27 that true religion is caring for widows and orphans and keeping ourselves from being stained by the world. Widows and orphans were some of the most vulnerable members of society in the ancient world. If a husband died, the widow and her children would generally not be able to sustain themselves. There were very few jobs for women and no support from the state, and inheritance laws provided few if any benefits for widows. Thus, if a woman's husband died, she also lost her livelihood and her social standing; she and her children were usually left in a dire economic situation and subject to exploitation.

Widows and orphans (the fatherless) are mentioned often throughout the Old Testament—from the books of Moses through the Prophets. From each passage noted, list all the groups of people mentioned that readers are called to care for and not oppress.

Deuteronomy 10:18-19	Deuteronomy 27:14, 19	Job 29:11-17	Job 31:16-22

Psalm 146:7-9	Isaiah 1:17	Jeremiah 7:1-8	Zechariah 7:8-14

What groups are most frequently mentioned in these passages?

_____

_____

_____

_____

While James particularly mentions widows and orphans, he is recalling the many places in the Old Testament where these and other oppressed or disadvantaged groups are mentioned. He's not intentionally excluding the poor, the needy, the imprisoned or foreigners in favor of widows and orphans. Rather he uses "widows and orphans" as a kind of shorthand to recall all of these different kinds of marginalized people that the Old Testament commonly considers together. It is for this group, says James, that we have responsibilities to fulfill.

[1]Robert W. Wall, "James, Letter of," in *Dictionary of the Later New Testament & Its Developments,* ed. Ralph P. Martin and Peter H. Davids (Downers Grove, IL: InterVarsity Press, 1997), p. 558.
[2]David P. Nystrom, *James,* The NIV Application Commentary (Grand Rapids: Zondervan, 1997), p. 91.

PART 3. REFLECT
Words to Live By

We once witnessed a domestic disturbance that became so intense that the police were called.

For months Bill had been acting erratically, impulsively—driving recklessly, coming home in the early hours of the morning, never explaining where he had been, stealing money he didn't need. His wife, Helen, was concerned that her husband could hurt himself or others. She wanted Bill to get help, but he refused.

The two of us were with Bill and Helen when his anger started to bubble. Believing things had reached a crisis point after so many increasingly dangerous episodes, Helen called the police. Soon several cars with flashing lights pulled up in front of the house. Two officers came to the door and Helen let them in. Together they found Bill in the family room. Seeing the uniformed police, Bill became even more agitated. He began using foul and insulting language, making extreme accusations against Helen.

Immediately one of the officers spoke up. "Sir," he said firmly and respectfully, "you may not use that language here. I don't know if your wife puts up with that when it's just the two of you, but you may not talk to her that way while I am here. If you have something to say to her or to us, as long as I am here, you will do so without talking like that."

Using this approach, the police skillfully kept a lid on a potentially volatile situation. Because they were able to exercise authority over Bill's words, they were able to exercise calm authority over his actions without resorting to anger themselves or the use of force. In essence, by controlling Bill's speech, the police did not need to use physical coercion to control what Bill did or didn't do. As a result, after some intense discussions, Bill agreed to go to a hospital.

Bill needed an external presence to control his words and, because of their close connection, his actions. James calls on us to "humbly accept the word planted in you, which can save you" (1:21). As a result of this internal presence, our words, and therefore our actions as well, will be under the authority of God.

According to James, words are central to who we are and what we do. The words we say can reveal our inner character. The words we take in and dwell on can likewise shape that inner character. Keeping our words under control is a key to our whole life being well ordered.

For James, the words that we are to listen to in particular are God's words. In James 1:12 he first introduced the theme of the importance of God's Word when he alludes to Psalm 1: "Blessed is the one . . . whose delight is in the law of the LORD, and who meditates on his law day and night. That person is like a tree planted by streams of water, which yields its fruit in season and whose leaf does not wither—whatever they do prospers." Now in 1:18 James reminds us that God "chose to give us birth through the word of truth."

In 1:19 he continues by telling us to be quick to hear this word. James's advice to be quick to hear, slow to speak and slow to become angry is certainly apt for us in any situation when dealing with family, friends, coworkers, neighbors and others. But what James has in mind, as the context makes clear, is being quick to listen to God's Word, slow to speak God's Word and slow to become angry on the basis of God's Word. We will see each of these three themes expanded in turn in James 2–4.

In 1:22 he begins to go more in depth on the first of these three themes. Listening to, really hearing God's Word, means that we allow it to shape our character, that we meditate on it so it becomes integral to who we are, to all we do and all we say. When we let God's Word have this effect, our words will reflect that inner reality. And that inner reality will then shape our outward behavior. It's a self-reinforcing cycle. We meditate on God's Word. That shapes our internal world, which shapes how we act. How we act then guides us back to God's Word, which then reinforces the form of our inner world.

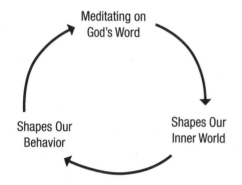

This cycle—the sense that there is to be harmony, unity and inner consistency between our inner and outer worlds—is a holistic Jewish idea rooted in the Old Testament and in Jesus. The two worlds are integrated, each consistently reflecting the other—for good or for ill. Our inner world (whether it is one that serves God or not) will eventually display itself in our outer world. When inner and outer worlds are at odds with each other and inconsistent, something is deeply wrong. Hearing without doing is self-deception (1:22).

It is all too easy to have a divided life. We see it even among active Christians. Some know the Word of God well, study it often, memorize it faithfully. But they fall short in doing the Word. Other Christians are exemplary in how they seek justice, aid the foreigner, and care for the poor and oppressed. But they do so with scant knowledge, awareness or concern for God's Word. Both kinds of Christians miss the full life in Christ that James is concerned about.

Without an inner life that dwells on God's Word and draws on his power, activists can become burned out, cynical and uncaring. When they see the failures of human nature all around them and realize they can't solve all the world's problems, it is all too tempting to give up even the good work they are involved in.

On the flip side, without a life that expresses God's love to people in tangible ways—feeding the hungry, visiting prisoners, seeking to right wrongs done to widows and orphans, helping the foreigner and stranger—we can become self-righteous in our knowledge and ultimately cold toward God. If we don't show love toward our neighbors, our love for God becomes dead legalism.

In James 1:1-18, we saw that wisdom is not just an inner quality of being smart or clever. It includes the dimension of knowing and doing the just thing. Likewise, hearing the Word means deeply grafting it into our lives in a way that expresses itself in practical, gritty love for those in need.

What's the main idea in this section?

What is one thing you can act on based on this reading?

PART 4. DISCUSS
Putting It All Together

OPEN

Think about a situation in which you were not pleased with how you listened to someone. Think of another situation in which you were not pleased with how someone listened to you. Why is it so difficult to be a good listener?

READ JAMES 1:19-27.

We all do it. It is as common as flies around a horse. While someone else is talking, we're thinking about what we are going to say next instead of considering what is being said to us. We know that others are worth more care and attention. But the habit is hard to break.

God wants us to slow down and listen to him too. But even when we've really listened to him, we're still not done.

1. In verse 19 James commands his readers to "be quick to listen, slow to speak and slow to become angry." Why are these three commands relevant in the context of trials and temptations?

2. Under the heading "Be Quick to Hear" in part two, we considered Psalms 1:1-3 and 19:7-10. What do they tell us about how people are transformed when they internalize God's Word in a deep way?

3. An exercise in part two lists Old Testament passages that describe the positive results of being slow to speak and the negative results of being quick to speak. How have you experienced any of those results in yourself and in others?

4. In part two, "Connect: Scripture to Scripture," we saw that Jesus takes anger seriously in the Sermon on the Mount. We also looked at passages about anger from the book of Proverbs. What principles about anger from Proverbs struck you most and why?

5. What steps could you take to grow as a person who is slow to anger, quick to hear or slow to speak?

6. In part two we said that James's story of looking in a mirror and forgetting what we look like is similar to hearing the Word and not doing it. It's giving "lip service" to the importance of God's Word but not taking it seriously in how we live our lives. What examples did you write down of how we give lip service to God's Word?

7. According to 1:26-27, how does James's criteria for true religion compare to and contrast with what is considered proof of authentic belief today?

8. When James tells us to care for "widows and orphans," the most vulnerable of society in that day, he means for us to care for all disadvantaged and oppressed people. Who are the "widows and orphans" in your life or community?

9. To truly hear the Word means to deeply graft it into our lives in a way that expresses practical, gritty love for those in need. What step can you take to care for the "widows and orphans" that you have identified?

10. The reading in part three emphasizes the importance of having harmony between our inner and outer worlds. What dangers have you seen in not having consistency between these aspects of our lives?

11. Based on what you have read in this chapter, do you think that James would be satisfied with good works apart from our hearing and receiving God's Word? Explain.

12. As you think back over chapter 1 of James, what have you learned about what God desires from us?

Spend some time in silence. Listen to discover what voices and messages are on your mind. After a few minutes, pray together out loud about those things that distract you from him. Pray for each other—that the Holy Spirit will clear your mind and help you focus on him.

WHO'S THE JUDGE?

James 2:1-13

WHERE WE'RE GOING

For James, as in the Old Testament, truly *hearing* God's Word means also *doing* God's Word. As we saw at the very conclusion of the Sermon on the Mount, Jesus says, "Therefore everyone who hears these words of mine and puts them into practice is like a wise man who built his house on the rock" (Matthew 7:24). Hearing and putting into practice are inseparable. They together are wisdom.

In 2:1-13, James continues his first major theme of being "quick to hear" in this very active sense. In particular, he wants his readers to hear and therefore act in ways that don't show bias or prejudice to others based on human, worldly standards. That's not the way God operates, and neither should we.

Part 1. Investigate: James 2:1-13 (On Your Own)

Part 2. Connect: Scripture to Scripture (On Your Own)

Part 3. Reflect: Rich and Poor (On Your Own)

Part 4. Discuss: Putting It All Together (With a Group)

A PRAYER TO PRAY

Jesus Christ, Lord of Glory, we praise you that you have chosen the poor, the weak and the powerless of this world to be rich in faith and to inherit your kingdom. We give thanks that you are a just Judge who is completely impartial and fair when dealing with everyone. We ask, therefore, that you will make us like you, that we might show compassion and give aid to those who are in need or in debt or who have no claim to favorable treatment. We ask this so that your mercy will shine through us to the whole world, in order that all might praise you. Amen.

PART 1. INVESTIGATE
James 2:1-13

1. Read James 2:1-13. What are some results of showing favoritism (vv. 4, 6, 9, 13)?

2. Why should believing in "our glorious Lord Jesus Christ" (v. 1) keep us from showing favoritism?

3. How would you react if someone came into your church who wore sloppy clothes, was dirty or had body odor (vv. 2-4)?

4. Why do many people give preferential treatment to those who have money?

5. Verse 5 says God has chosen the poor to be rich in faith. Is God guilty of showing favoritism in this way? Explain.

6. Is it easier to have faith when you are poor than when you are rich? Explain.

7. From a practical standpoint, why was it foolish for early Christians to favor the rich over the poor (vv. 6-7)?

2:2. *Moralists and satirists mocked the special respect given to the wealthy, which usually amounted to a self-demeaning way to seek funds. Illustrations like this one could be hypothetical, which fit the writer's diatribe style of argument. In Rome the senatorial class wore gold rings; some members of this class sought popular support for favors shown to various groups. But rings were hardly limited to them; in the eastern Mediterranean gold rings also marked great wealth and status. Clothing likewise distinguished the wealthy, who could be ostentatious, from others; peasants commonly had only one cloak, which would thus often be dirty.*

"Assembly" (KJV, NASB, NRSV) or "meeting" (NIV, TEV) is literally "synagogue," either because James wants the whole Jewish community to embrace his example, or because the Jewish-Christian congregations (cf. 5:14) also considered themselves messianic synagogues.

2:6. *Roman courts always favored the rich, who could initiate lawsuits against social inferiors, although social inferiors could not initiate lawsuits against them. In theory, Jewish courts sought to avoid this discrimination, but as in most cultures people of means naturally had legal advantages: they were able to argue their cases more articulately or to hire others to do so for them.*

2:9-10. *Jewish teachers distinguished "heavier" from "lighter" sins, but felt that God required obedience to even the "smallest" command-ments, rewarding the obedient with eternal life and punishing transgressors with damnation. That willful violation of even a minor transgression was tantamount to rejecting the whole law was one of their most commonly repeated views. (Ancient writers often stated principles in sharp, graphic ways but in practice showed more mercy to actual transgressors in the community.)*

Stoics (against the Epicure-ans) went even farther in declaring that all sins were equal. The point here is that rejecting the law of economic impartiality in Leviticus 19:15, or the general principle of love behind it (Lev 19:18), was rejecting the whole authority of God (Jas 2:8).

How is James's description of the rich valid today?

8. How can "the royal law" (v. 8) guide our treatment of both poor and rich?

9. How do verses 9-11 emphasize the seriousness of treating people unequally?

10. In what sense is violating one law as serious as breaking every law?

11. What happens to those who show mercy and those who do not (vv. 12-13)?

12. The cross is the ultimate example of mercy triumphing over judgment. How has the mercy you have received there af-fected the way you interact with others?

Think of ways in which you show favoritism. Ask God to help you change your attitudes and actions.

PART 2. CONNECT
Scripture to Scripture

OUR GLORIOUS LORD JESUS CHRIST

Twice James invokes the name of Jesus in his letter—at the very beginning and here at the beginning of chapter 2. This time he calls Jesus "our glorious Lord." *Glory* is a word that is often associated with great splendor and radiance, with displays of magnificent power and greatness—so it makes sense that, in the Old Testament, *glory* is often associated with God's presence, especially when we consider how often God made his presence *visible* to the Israelites. Look up the passages below and fill in the blanks.

Exodus 24:15-18

When Moses went up on the mountain, the _____ covered it, and the _____ of the LORD settled on Mount Sinai. For six days the _____ covered the mountain, and on the seventh day the LORD called to Moses from within the _____. To the Israelites the _____ of the LORD looked like a consuming fire on top of the mountain. Then Moses entered the _____ as he went on up the mountain. And he stayed on the mountain forty days and forty nights.

Exodus 40:34-38

Then the _____ covered the tent of meeting, and the _____ of the LORD filled the tabernacle. Moses could not enter the tent of meeting because the _____ had settled on it, and the _____ of the LORD filled the tabernacle.

In all the travels of the Israelites, whenever the _____ lifted from above the tabernacle, they would set out; but if the _____ did not lift, they did not set out—until the day it lifted. So the _____ of the LORD was over the tabernacle by day, and fire was in the _____ by night, in the sight of all the Israelites during all their travels.

Matthew 17:1-8

After six days Jesus took with him Peter, James and John the brother of James, and led them up a high mountain by themselves. There he was transfigured before them. His face shone like the sun, and his clothes became as white as the light. Just then there appeared before them Moses and Elijah, talking with Jesus.

Peter said to Jesus, "Lord, it is good for us to be here. If you wish, I will put up three shelters—one for you, one for Moses and one for Elijah."

While he was still speaking, a bright _____ covered them, and a voice from the _____ said, "This is my Son, whom I love; with him I am well pleased. Listen to him!"

When the disciples heard this, they fell facedown to the ground, terrified. But Jesus came and touched them. "Get up," he said. "Don't be afraid." When they looked up, they saw no one except Jesus.

Though James doesn't claim to actually be able to see God's presence as a cloud, he clearly has a sense of the reality of God—in all his magnificence—with him and with those he's writing to. Essentially, when James describes Jesus as "glorious" he is emphasizing that his divine presence is with his people.

There is another key passage in the book of Exodus that helps us understand what the Bible means by *glory*. In Exodus 32 Moses faces a major crisis after leading the people of Israel out of slavery in Egypt. He had been gone so long on Mount Sinai to meet with God that the people were afraid he'd never come back. Feeling vulnerable and in need of divine protection, they made an idol to worship in the form of a golden calf.

God was disgusted by their lack of faithfulness to him. So in Exodus 33 he tells Moses that they can still go to the Promised Land, but they'll have to go without God's presence; if he were to go with them, he explains, he might destroy them because of their appalling disobedience. Moses pleads with God on behalf of the people, however, and because God is pleased with Moses, he agrees to go with them to the Promised Land. Then Moses makes a bold request in 33:18: "Show me your glory."

Read God's response to this in Exodus 33:19–34:7. What do we learn here about what God's glory means in addition to his presence?

_____

_____

_____

_____

This fills in with even more detail what James has in mind when he calls Jesus glorious. What is the significance of this in light of James's topic in 2:1-13?

_____

_____

_____

_____

PLAYING FAVORITES

James 1 ends with an exhortation to not be polluted or stained by the world. What did he mean by that? James offers an example in his very next sentence, right at the beginning of chapter 2—showing favoritism to the rich over the poor. That's the way of the world. Money speaks, as we say. But that's not to be the way of God's people. This is a theme that goes deeply into the roots of the Old Testament.

Read Job 34:16-20 and paraphrase what it says about how God regards partiality and impartiality.

_____

_____

Now read the laws in the following verses given to Moses for the nation of Israel after they left Egypt: Leviticus 19:15 and Deuteronomy 1:16-17; 16:18-20. How were judges to do their work when dealing with different kinds of people?

_____

_____

_____

_____

God didn't just instruct judges regarding impartiality, though; he prescribed parameters for the daily life of the Israelites that would keep all of them from showing favoritism.

Read Leviticus 25:8-13, 23-24, 35-38. What were the structures that God put into the societal fabric of ancient Israel to keep people out of poverty?

_____

_____

_____

_____

What are the ways that society today favors the rich and makes life easier for them?

_____

_____

_____

_____

How do churches today sometimes show favoritism toward rich people?

_____

_____

_____

_____

Once again we see the influence of the Sermon on the Mount on James's thoughts and words. Read Matthew 7:1-5. What, according to these verses, is problematic about judging others?

_____

_____

GOD HAS CHOSEN THE POOR

In James 2:5, we read that God has chosen the poor for a special blessing. We often think of God's election of people as something that applies primarily to individuals. Here a whole group benefits.

Likewise, in the Old Testament there is an emphasis on election concerning large groups (not necessarily regarding salvation but regarding other blessings).

Many passages speak of God's election of the nation of Israel (see, e.g., Deuteronomy 4:37-38 and 14:2). But look especially at Deuteronomy 7:7-8. What themes do you find here that are similar to those in James 2:5?

_____

_____

_____

_____

Once again, the influence of Jesus' teaching from the Sermon on the Mount and elsewhere is evident. How are Matthew 5:3, 5 and 19:23-26 similar to James's thought in 2:5-7?

_____

_____

_____

_____

Why are the poor more likely to be rich in faith than the rich?

_____

_____

_____

_____

Circle the option below that best describes how your financial situation has affected your faith.
a. My financial situation has helped my faith grow.
b. My financial situation has hindered trusting God.
c. My financial situation has not had much effect on my faith.
Explain your answer.

_____

_____

_____

_____

THE NAME

Because Jews wanted to be sure they did not, even accidentally, break the commandment about taking the Lord's name in vain, they refrained from saying his name at all. Instead they used a number of substitutes for the divine name of *Yahweh*, most commonly, "the LORD." Another is

"Ancient of Days," found in Daniel 7:9, 13 and 22. "Heaven" is also be used for God, as when the prodigal son says he "sinned against heaven," by which he means he sinned against God.

"The name" (found in James 2:7) is still another. We find a couple Old Testament examples of this in Deuteronomy 28:10 and Isaiah 43:6-7. How are God's chosen identified with God himself?

_____

_____

_____

_____

Now look up Amos 2:6-7. How does this help explain why James thinks being unjust to the weak and powerless is a kind of blasphemy?

_____

_____

_____

_____

LOVING GOD AND NEIGHBOR

James 1:25 mentions "the perfect law that gives freedom," which is referred to again in 2:12. In 2:8 James makes explicit what he has in mind when he quotes directly from Leviticus 19:18, calling this "the royal law found in Scripture."

Why does he single out Leviticus 19:18? Clearly it's because of the heavy influence Jesus' teaching had on James.

When Jesus was asked once what the greatest commandment is, he not surprisingly mentioned loving God with all your heart, soul and strength, which is part of the Shema from Deuteronomy 6:4-5, a prayer recited daily by Jews. What *is* surprising, though, is that he attached Leviticus 19:18 to the Shema (see Mark 12:28-34).

Why is it impossible to separate loving God from loving your neighbor?

_____

_____

_____

_____

Read Matthew 5:17-22, 27-28. How do you see Jesus' influence in James 2:10-11?

_____

_____

_____

Given what Jesus says about murder, how might James (in a parallel way) think his readers are also actually guilty of murder?

_____

_____

_____

_____

MERCY TRIUMPHS OVER JUDGMENT

Mercy is a word that we may have run across so many times in the Bible that we lose a sense of its meaning. It's time to revisit Exodus 34:5-7, which we began this section with. Look also at Zechariah 7:8-10. Check all the items below that are found in these two passages and that apply as descriptions of *mercy*. (Don't check those which may be ways to show mercy unless they are found in one of these two passages.)

- ☐ Not tipping justice in favor of the rich
- ☐ Forgiving those who wrong you
- ☐ Not punishing people as they deserve
- ☐ Showing compassion to others
- ☐ Being patient with others
- ☐ Not being quick to judge the sins of others
- ☐ Not doing things that harm or hold down the poor or powerless
- ☐ Acting like others didn't do bad things
- ☐ Being generous to others
- ☐ Not devising ways to harm others

Many churches have had major conflicts about worship styles—traditional, contemporary, liturgical, blended. A lot of time, energy and emotion have been spent on these issues and debates. It's been so important to some that churches have split over such disagreements. The Old Testament prophets had a striking perspective on how important "worship" is in relation to other priorities. What particular forms of worship do Hosea 6:6 and Micah 6:6-8 mention?

_____

_____

What should our priorities be as Christian communities?

_____

_____

_____

_____

What more do we learn about mercy in the Sermon on the Mount, especially in Matthew 5:7 and 6:14-15?

_____

_____

_____

Mercy is, as the *Dictionary of Biblical Imagery* says, "compassion in action. . . . The Hebrew word *hesed* is often translated as 'mercy,' but is also translated as 'lovingkindness' and 'goodness.' . . . Mercy is aid rendered to someone who is miserable or needy, especially someone who is either in debt or without claim to favorable treatment."[1]

James was writing not just to individuals but to a whole community. He would not be satisfied if we, as his readers, failed to ask ourselves, "To whom should we be showing mercy and in what ways?" How would you answer that personally? How would your community answer that?

_____

_____

_____

_____

_____

When James speaks of judgment, he's not thinking of "final judgment" but of what God thinks about the sins of partiality and of taking advantage of the poor and powerless. And God has very strong views about this. We can rejoice, nonetheless, in the conclusion that James offers in 2:13, "Mercy triumphs over judgment."

How does this apply both to the situation of those who are powerless and to those who take advantage of the powerless?

_____

_____

_____

_____

For all of James's stern words, we should not mistake his priority as mere moralism, which can degenerate into legalism. The foundation of mercy is God's grace. The power of love is God's grace. We respond, listening to and obeying God's Word, not out of mere duty but with a heart of gratitude and love for the God who saved us in mercy.

[1]Leland Ryken, James C. Wilhoit and Tremper Longman, eds., *Dictionary of Biblical Imagery* (Downers Grove, IL: InterVarsity Press, 1998), pp. 547-48.

PART 3. REFLECT
Rich and Poor

Desperate for work, a single parent of three with no marketplace skills, Erin Brockovich took a low-paying job as a legal assistant in a California law firm. While going through some files for a real-estate deal, she couldn't figure out why they included medical records.

She soon discovered that the link between the real estate and the medical records was Pacific Gas and Electric (PG&E), the world's largest public utility. PG&E had contaminated the water supply of Hinkley, a town of about two thousand people in the high desert of southern California. The company had detected chrome 6 (a cancer-causing chemical) from its nearby compressor station as far back as 1965. And people had been getting sick. Over a period of decades PG&E had dumped 370 million gallons of chemicals into unlined ponds close by. Now the company was buying up land and destroying the buildings on them.

When Brockovich examined local water records and interviewed people who had become ill, her suspicions were confirmed. But how could a small law firm representing a small town possibly succeed in bringing legal action against the multi-billion-dollar behemoth?

Brockovich persisted. Against his own instincts, her boss agreed to take on the case. In 1993 the firm filed suit against PG&E on behalf of 77 plaintiffs; the number eventually grew to 648. After years of providing misinformation to the town, the company now fought back. But the lawyers for the town compelled the company to produce relevant documents. As one of the plaintiffs told a reporter, "They thought they were dealing with a bunch of dumb hicks, that's what I think."

Financially, however, the law firm was stretched beyond its limits. Personally, Erin spent so much time on the case that she began to lose touch with her kids. After uncertainty and setbacks, the judge finally found in favor of the town and awarded the residents a settlement of $333 million.

The story was made into one of Hollywood's most inspirational movies, *Erin Brockovich*. When a passionate single mom with no legal training and a small town without resources triumph over a huge, powerful corporation that has taken advantage of them for years, we can't help but cheer.

Unfortunately, the flip side—the story of the powerful overwhelming the weak—is all too common. It may be a dictator who enriches himself at the cost of impoverishing his own people. Or it may be a family whose house is foreclosed by a bank who won't renegotiate a reasonable mortgage payment.

The rich and the poor do not operate on a level playing field. The rich have the power to influence lawmaking in their favor, to apply financial pressure where needed to get their way, and to hint at potential benefits for those who support them. The poor have none of this. And so it has been through the centuries, as it was when James wrote his letter to fellow believers in Jesus Christ.

James offers several reasons why favoring the rich makes no sense. On the practical side, they are the ones taking advantage of most of his readers. On the theological side, God is the source of compassion, graciousness, patience, love, faithfulness and forgiveness. As people who are called by his name, who have his very being stamped in our hearts, so should we also be. This is especially the case when we deal with those who have few resources or little influence in society—whether they be orphans, those among us from other countries, the homeless or the unemployed.

God instructed ancient Israel to institute a society-wide system for ensuring that whole groups of people were not permanently impoverished. This was the Year of Jubilee, to be held once every fifty years. Leviticus 25 prescribes that all land sold since the previous Year of Jubilee was to be returned to the previous owners. In the economics of the day, those without land had no means of independent income, so returning land to the original families was essential to maintain widespread economic well-being. With this model in mind, it is not inappropriate today for us to consider and support society-wide options for keeping large groups of people out of poor and oppressed conditions.

The early church took James's message seriously. As Rodney Stark points out in *The Rise of Christianity,* when plagues hit the Roman Empire in A.D. 165 and 251, instead of fleeing the towns as the (mostly rich) pagans did, Christians (rich and poor) stayed to help both fellow Christians and pagans who were unable to leave. Their lived message of love and self-sacrifice for the weak of society had a profound impact on the Empire. So much so that within three hundred years after the death of Jesus, approximately half the population of the Empire had become Christians.

For these early Christians, there was no division between "acts of mercy" and the "good news of Jesus." They were one in the same. After all, as Jesus taught and James repeated, loving God and loving others must go together.

There are, of course, many possible options for how we might do this. Here's just one example—a way our church has sought to live out our love for God and others. Because the suburbs we're in have a large Hispanic population nearby, we have occasionally, in conjunction with a Hispanic congregation that meets in our building Sunday afternoons, offered free medical clinics staffed largely by doctors and nurses and others from our church. Our aim is to meet the physical needs of a large group of people who do not have other safety nets to fall back on while also seeking to draw them into a community that can meet their spiritual needs.

James's negative exhortation is clear: do not favor the rich. But there is also a positive challenge for us as believers today: find ways to honor the poor as those made in God's image. In this way we show for all to see how the mercy of our glorious Lord Jesus Christ triumphs over judgment.

What's the main idea in this section?

What is one thing you can act on based on this reading?

PART 4. DISCUSS
Putting It All Together

OPEN

What kinds of things make you favor one person more than another?

READ JAMES 2:1-13.

Labels are found in more places than on soup cans. We put them on people all the time. Funny or dull. Smart or thickheaded. Friendly or cold. There are all kinds of ways we can categorize people. And our categories can have a profound influence on the way we treat people.

1. James 1 ends with an exhortation to not be polluted or stained by the world. James offers an example of this at the beginning of chapter 2. To show favoritism to the rich over the poor is the way of the world. What example of favoritism does he give (vv. 2-3)?

2. *Glory* is a word that is often associated with great splendor and radiance, with displays of God's magnificent power and greatness. In the Old Testament, *glory* is frequently associated with God's presence. Why do you think James calls Jesus "our glorious Lord Jesus Christ" when speaking against showing favoritism?

3. What examples did you write down in part two, "Connect: Scripture to Scripture," for the ways that society today favors the rich and makes life easier for them?

4. As you've gone through this study, what has God revealed to you about favoritism you or your church might be showing toward a particular group of people?

5. In verses 5-12 what reasons are given for why insulting the poor is so problematic?

6. Why did James write that those who are poor in the eyes of the world are rich in faith?

7. How does your financial situation affect your faith?

8. In Old Testament times the name of God was held with such high regard that the Jews would not speak it. James said the rich "slander the noble name of him to whom you belong." How are you affected when you hear the noble name of God being slandered?

9. Why is showing favoritism breaking the law of God (vv. 8-11)?

10. As we read in part two, mercy is "compassion in action. . . . The Hebrew word *hesed* is often translated as 'mercy,' but is also translated as 'lovingkindness' and 'goodness.' . . . Mercy is aid rendered to someone who is miserable or needy, especially someone who is either in debt or without claim to favorable treatment." We also looked at Exodus 34:5-7 and Zechariah 7:8-10 to gain more insight into the term *mercy*.

    How has your concept of mercy expanded as a result of this study?

11. Why is the concept of mercy so important in this passage?

12. What would a modern-day Year of Jubilee look like?

13. How can your Christian community show mercy to the weak and poor in your sphere of influence?

Spend some time together confessing ways that you individually and your church community as a whole have shown favoritism. Ask for God's forgiveness and then for help in finding ways to honor the poor as those made in God's image. Invite the Holy Spirit to show from your life how the mercy of our glorious Lord Jesus Christ triumphs over judgment.

SESSION FOUR

JUST WORKS

James 2:14-26

WHERE WE'RE GOING

Mark Twain is noted for his wry comment, "It ain't those parts of
the Bible that I can't understand that bother me, it is the parts
that I do understand." Many places in the Bible are exceedingly
clear about what God expects us to do and not to do—and often
we don't like what we find.

The book of James is one of those places in Scripture. In his letter
James is remarkably straightforward about how he expects those
who believe in Jesus to act. And don't try to hide behind your theology, he cautions. That won't save you. It's much deeper than that.

   Part 1. Investigate: James 2:14-26 (On Your Own)

   Part 2. Connect: Scripture to Scripture (On Your Own)

   Part 3. Reflect: Faith Is Never Alone (On Your Own)

   Part 4. Discuss: Putting It All Together (With a Group)

A PRAYER TO PRAY

*Father, Son and Spirit, you are the one true God we worship. You are
the one who promised to Abraham that through him and his seed, all
the nations of the earth would be blessed. Your charge to him and to
everyone who follows in his footsteps of faith is to fulfill that calling—to be a channel of grace and mercy to every nation and race,
near and far. We ask, therefore, that we might be true heirs of the
promise to Abraham, people who express our faith through love for
those who have less, for those who are strangers from other countries, and for those who are our brothers and sisters in Christ. We
ask that you would do this in order that we might be called your
friends—for our good, for the good of your church and for the good
of the whole world. Amen.*

PART 1. INVESTIGATE
James 2:14-26

Read James 2:14-26.

2:15-16. *"Go in peace" was a Jewish farewell blessing, but Jewish people were expected to show hospitality to other Jewish people in need. "Be warmed" (NASB) alludes to how cold the homeless could become, especially in a place of high elevation like Jerusalem in winter.*

1. Retell in your own words James's mini-parable in 2:15-17.

2. What would be an example of someone doing something today like what is described in 2:15-17?

3. James states clearly here that faith without works is dead. What opportunity do you have to show your faith by caring for those in need?

4. Why is mere intellectual agreement to truth not enough, according to James (v. 19)?

2:21-24. *James connects Genesis 15:6 with the offering of Isaac (Gen 22), as in Jewish tradition. This event was the climax of his faith in God, not only in Jewish tradition but in the Genesis narrative itself. Abraham was "declared righteous" at the Aqedah, the offering of Isaac, in the sense that God again acknowledged (Gen 22:12) Abraham's prior faith, which had been tested ultimately at this point. The Old Testament called Abraham God's friend (2 Chron 20:7; Is 41:8), and later Jewish writers delighted in this title for him.*

5. The story of Abraham taking his young son Isaac up the mountain to sacrifice him (Genesis 22) is one of the better known episodes in the Old Testament. Which part of this story from Abraham's life strikes you most strongly?

6. Why would James say that Abraham's faith was made complete by what he did (vv. 21-24)?

7. Describe a time in your life or from the life of someone you

know when obedience to God was or could have been at great
personal cost.

8. The story of Rahab is told in Joshua 2 and 6. How did Rahab's
   belief affect her (v. 25)?

9. How are your actions guided and empowered by the reality of
   your faith?

10. How does James's closing analogy (v. 26) summarize his
    teaching on faith and actions?

11. James never says that works without faith can save. What
    does this imply about faith?

12. In what ways do you need to bring your actions more in line
    with your beliefs?

*Reflect on your life in the past seven to ten days. Write down situa-
tions in which what you did or said or thought did not match up with
what you believe. Ask God to forgive you, change you and make you
more like him. Then write down situations in which you clearly lived
out what you believe. Thank God for his faithful work in your life.*

PART 2. CONNECT
Scripture to Scripture

BE WARMED AND FILLED

Andy was chatting with a friend once, Bill, who had taken a new job with a multi-billion-dollar corporation. He had been hired to lead the conversion of the entire company's business software system to a new package. This was an immense job. Bill knew full well that some companies had gone into bankruptcy or had to be sold off because of a failed conversion. He found the challenge at once exciting and frightening.

Since Andy had no expertise in business technology whatsoever, he responded with a half smile and said, "Well, Bill, be warmed and filled." They both laughed, recognizing the reference to James 2:16. It was shorthand for saying, "You're on your own on this one, buddy. I can't help you one bit. It's way out of my league. You got yourself in this mess, and you're going to have to get yourself out."

Andy couldn't help Bill at all, and could joke about it, but in a similar vein, James shows us how ridiculous it is to merely wish someone well when we *can* help them—to stand by or walk on in the face of an obvious need they have that we can remedy! It's like watching someone labor alone to fix a flat tire or to prepare a meal for a large group and saying, "I wish there were someone here to help you."

James 2:15-16 might be humorous too if it weren't so serious. Packed into those verses is a long tradition of ethical teaching with roots deep in the Old Testament, which James is drawing on.

In Job 24, for example, Job complains to God that the wicked seem to prosper at the expense of the weak. Why doesn't God come in judgment on them? Why doesn't he do something about this? These are difficult and important questions which are addressed in Job and elsewhere in the Bible. While we don't have time to consider them here, we can look at Job 24 to get a picture of what unrighteous and unethical behavior looked like in the view of the ancient Hebrews.

Read Job 24:1-12 and make two lists—one of the wrong things the wicked do and another listing aspects of how the weak and poor live. We helped you get started on both lists.

What the Wicked Do	What the Weak Do
Move landmarks (cheat on property)	Hide themselves

As Job seeks to justify himself against the accusations of his so-called friends, he catalogs his righteous behavior. So in Job 31 we get a similar picture of the ethical world of ancient Israel. Read Job 31:16-23 and list things moral people would be expected to do or to refrain from doing.

_____   _____

_____   _____

_____   _____

_____   _____

_____   _____

Isaiah reinforces this perspective. In Isaiah 58:6-9 he contrasts "spiritual" activity like fasting with caring for those in need. The prophet is using exaggeration to make a point. Of course it is fine and helpful to fast as a spiritual discipline. But if we fast and pray and read the Bible daily yet don't help those with fewer resources in society—then our spirituality is empty. But to do them is to receive God's blessing.

Read Isaiah 58:6-9. List the things Isaiah says are the activities God desires and the blessings he offers.

The Activities God Desires	The Blessings God Offers

James reminds his readers that as followers of Jesus we are not excused from these expressions of God's will. Because of his glorious grace, we are to live out a life worthy of our calling in Christ. Thinking over the lists you've made from Job and Isaiah, what are the chains of injustice that need to be loosened in your community or country?

_____

_____

_____

_____

What is one step you could take this week to participate in freeing those who do not have the support structures of society that others abundantly enjoy?

_____

_____

_____

_____

FAITH AND WORKS

Saying we believe God exists is not the same thing as loving him, James reminds us in 2:19; even the demons believe that. Those who were familiar with Jesus' ministry would not be surprised at James saying the demons shudder when they consider the one God. Read Matthew 8:28-34. How do the demons react to Jesus?

_____

_____

When it comes to what our works reveal about our relationship with God, James again follows the teachings of Jesus (as in the rest of his letter). Read Matthew 7:15-20. How, according to Jesus, will we know a false prophet from a true prophet?

_____

_____

_____

_____

What further light does this shed on James's words about faith and works?

_____

_____

_____

Now consider Matthew 25:31-46. How are the deeds that the Son of Man expects from his followers similar to what we saw in Job 31, Isaiah 58 and James 2?

_____

_____

_____

In 2:19 James offers another response to those who think merely having right doctrine is adequate in God's mind. He references Deuteronomy 6:4, "Hear, O Israel: The LORD our God, the LORD is one." This is the Shema we have mentioned before, the central prayer and creed repeated several times a day by observant Hebrews. It includes the next verse in Deuteronomy as well: "Love the LORD your God with all your heart and with all your soul and with all your strength."

As we saw previously, one of the radical moves that Jesus made in the context of first-century Judaism was to alter the Shema, this central core of Jewish faith (Matthew 22:34-40). How does James's teaching about faith and works parallel Jesus' answer to the question posed to him in Matthew 22?

_____

_____

_____

_____

In the course of his letter James covers all the major points of these two Great Commandments that Jesus draws from the Old Testament (Deuteronomy 6:4-5 and Leviticus 19:18). Write down the different elements from these two commandments found in each of the following passages from James as we have done for 1:12 and circle the verse it refers to.

James 1:12 _____Love God_____ From (circle one): Deut 6:4; Deut 6:5; or Lev 19:18

James 2:5 _____ From (circle one) Deut 6:4; Deut 6:5; or Lev 19:18

James 2:8 _____ From (circle one): Deut 6:4; Deut 6:5; or Lev 19:18

James 2:19 _____ From (circle one): Deut 6:4; Deut 6:5; or Lev 19:18

Jesus inextricably links loving God and loving others. James follows the lead of his Lord by doing the same, by linking the call in Deuteronomy 6:4-5 to love the one God of the universe with the call in Leviticus 19:18 to love our neighbors. We love God for the matchless grace and mercy he has shown us, for his immense generosity in giving us everything we are and have, for saving us from ourselves, sin and death. We respond not out of obligation or a sense of duty—and certainly not out of fear of God's wrath or anger—but in a free act of gratitude. How? By willingly, cheerfully doing what God asks.

When a husband and wife love each other, it is not a burden or a chore to do what the other asks. It's a joy. We love to serve those we love. So we seek to fulfill the central thing God asks of us—to love others. And as James emphasizes, God wants us to be particularly aware of those in need.

If we have trouble loving others, we may well ask, then, do we love God? Do we truly understand and appreciate how he has given not only all things but his very self so that we can live—now and in the age to come?

_____

_____

_____

_____

How would you appraise your love for God?

_____

_____

_____

_____

ABRAHAM CONSIDERED RIGHTEOUS
To support his point that faith without works is useless, James offers two Old Testament examples. The first is Abraham, the father of Isaac and grandfather of Jacob. (See "The Twelve Tribes" in part two of session one.) Since Abraham was the father of the nation of Israel, an appeal to him would have had great weight in James's argument. In particular, in verses 21-22 of chapter 2 he focuses on the episode in which God asked Abraham to take Isaac to a mountain and sacrifice him there. Read the story in Genesis 22:1-19. Now retell the story below in your own words.

_____

_____

_____

_____

_____

_____

In verse 23, James then quotes Genesis 15:6. This Scripture was fulfilled, says James, when Abraham showed his faith in the episode with Isaac. Read the larger context of this passage in Genesis 15:1-6. What promises and blessings does God offer to Abram (later called Abraham)?

_____

_____

_____

_____

In the great chapter on faith in Hebrews 11, the author also combines Genesis 15 and 22 in the context of faith. What similarities do you see between Hebrews 11:17-19 and James 2:21-23?

_____

_____

_____

_____

What differences do you find between Hebrews 11:17-19 and James 2:21-23?

_____

_____

_____

_____

RAHAB THE PROSTITUTE

The second Old Testament example James offers is Rahab. Read her story in Joshua 2. Retell the story in your own words.

_____

_____

_____

_____

_____

_____

_____

The rest of the story when Israel conquers Jericho is then told in Joshua 6:15-25. What happened to Rahab and why?

_____

_____

_____

_____

In contrast to Abraham, the great patriarch of the Hebrew people, Rahab is a minor figure in the conquest story of the Promised Land. While Abraham was the father of the Hebrews, Rahab was a Canaanite Gentile. Abraham was a man; Rahab was a woman. Abraham had great wealth as a respected businessman; Rahab engaged in the disreputable profession of prostitution. Each of these pairs contrasts the high status of Abraham and the low status of Rahab. Yet James accords Rahab equal honor as a model of faith expressed in works. Why?

_____

_____

_____

_____

Israel as a nation and a culture placed a high value on hospitality. Read Exodus 22:21, Deuteronomy 10:17-19 and Leviticus 19:33-34. Why were the Israelites to offer hospitality to foreigners and strangers?

_____

_____

In ancient Israel, besides offering food and lodging, hosts were expected to provide protection. Genesis 19 relates the story of Lot attempting to protect the two strangers from the mob. He rightly felt obligated to give them protection as guests but notoriously offered his daughters to the mob as the means to do so (19:8). In 2 Kings 6:21-23 we read that even soldiers captured in war are to be given protection.

In 1 Samuel 25:1-13 and 33-36 we see the seriousness with which hospitality was regarded when we read of the potential dire consequences for blatant inhospitality. Nabal's wife Abigail, however, prevented David from slaughtering the whole household due to Nabal's insolence.

Hospitality was at the core of the identity of Israel as a nation. As Abraham symbolized the core of that identity, so, in a different way, did Rahab.

How does Rahab's example fit with James's exortations in 2:1-4 and 2:14-17?

_____

_____

_____

_____

James does not provide the only New Testament reference to Rahab. Read Matthew 1:1-6 and fill in the missing names.

Rahab was the mother of _____ [who is a main character in the book of Ruth, and himself an iconic example of hospitality].

Rahab was the grandmother of _____.

And she was the great grandmother of _____.

And the great, great grandmother of _____.

Rahab, a prostitute, was a hero of faith in action and an ancestor of Jesus. Hebrews 11:31 also considers Rahab a hero of faith for her hospitality.

◊ ◊ ◊

For James, faith and works are inseparable. The one without the other is as good as dead, and a phony. There are several kinds of phony faith, though. One is a faith that only expresses itself in lip service without truly fulfilling the royal law of loving God and neighbor. Another is a creed-only belief that acknowledges the reality of God but doesn't result in worship or obedience.

True faith, James shows us, is hearing that results in doing—hearing and doing in combination. True faith changes us from the inside out—heart, soul, mind, strength. Thus James concludes this section on being quick to hear God's Word. His main point? True faith is found in one who hears Jesus' words to love God and love neighbors and, in hearing, puts them into practice—like Abraham, like Rahab, like a wise man who built his house on a rock.

PART 3. REFLECT
Faith Is Never Alone

When the Reformation broke across Europe following Martin Luther's bold proclamation that we are saved by grace through faith and not by works, the authorities of the Catholic Church responded with strong arguments of their own. Weren't Luther and the other Reformers saying that godliness doesn't matter? How could they defend the idea that God doesn't care if we sin, that holy living is optional? What would motivate people to live upright lives?

The uproar was all unleashed in 1517 when Luther hammered his Ninety-Five Theses onto the door of the church in Wittenberg, protesting various teachings and practices of the Church. From that point forward, the Reformers consistently insisted on the doctrine of justification *sola fide*. It was by grace alone through faith that we could be made right with God—not by giving money to the church or engaging in acts of penitence or repeating formalized prayers. Luther had found the abuses regarding the buying of indulgences (giving money to the church in exchange for remission of sin and the punishment after death that went along with it) to be particularly objectionable.

No, insisted the Reformers, God's saving grace was bestowed on us freely through faith in him alone. As a monk, Luther had been haunted by the requirements of the Church, fearful that despite his most diligent efforts he was falling short of what God required. Then the truth of the gospel as taught by Paul in Romans 1:17 broke over him: "For in the gospel the righteousness of God is revealed—a righteousness that is by faith from first to last, just as it is written: 'The righteous will live by faith.'"

We cannot earn our salvation. Rather it is God's free gift to us when we trust in the death and resurrection of Jesus, who made a way for our sins to be forgiven. That's how we are reconciled to God. The apostle Paul confirmed this glorious truth in Galatians 2:16 when he wrote, "A person is not justified by the works of the law, but by faith in Jesus Christ. So we, too, have put our faith in Christ Jesus that we may be justified by faith in Christ and not by the works of the law, because by the works of the law no one will be justified." Neither Luther nor any of us need fear the wrath of God if we simply receive his grace by faith. What a glorious, liberating truth!

Yet, objected the defenders of the medieval teachings of the Catholic Church, this central teaching of the Reformation seemed to undercut any need to live a moral life. Were adultery, drunkenness, murder, stealing, anger and blasphemy now options for Christians? It didn't seem to matter what we did; we could still be saved by grace.

The Reformers were just as united in their response to this charge as they were in support of *sola fide*. One of Luther's staunchest supporters, Philip Melanchthon, responded to these challenges in 1531 by writing, "Our opponents slanderously claim that we do not require good works, whereas we not only require them but show how they can be done."[1] In *The Freedom of a Christian* Luther himself states that while works do not justify a person before God, a Christian "does the works out of spontaneous love in obedience to God and considers nothing except the approval of God, whom he would most scrupulously obey in all things."[2] John Calvin, Ulrich Zwingli, Martin Bucer and many other Reformers all strongly agreed.

The Reformation formula became, "We are justified by faith alone, but the faith that justifies is never alone." Justifying faith leads to good works, performed with love toward God and our neighbors, in grateful obedience to God. Faith that is alone, that does not show itself in good works, is no faith at all. As Jesus himself taught in Matthew, "By their fruit you will recognize them. Do people pick grapes from thornbushes, or figs from thistles?" (7:16), and "The mouth speaks what the heart is full of. A good man brings good things out of the good stored up in him, and an evil man brings evil things out of the evil stored up in him" (12:34-35).

James would thoroughly concur with the Reformers. Unfortunately, distortions of this truth have plagued the church in recent centuries. Too often the great message of salvation by faith has been truncated to just praying a prayer, raising a hand, walking the aisle. Such a gospel of cheap grace demeans the complete gospel of Jesus, who did not commission the apostles to make *converts* but to make *disciples* who would *obey* everything he taught (Matthew 28:19-20). Good works, empowered by the Holy Spirit and empowered by love as we grow in our faith, are evidence of a true surrender of all of who we are to Jesus.

Not too many years ago, one country in Africa was a model of the modern Christian missionary movement. The first missionary stations were established there in 1900; before the century was over, more than 90 percent of the country had become Christian. An astonishing success? Yes, except that the country was Rwanda, which in 1994 saw Rwandan Christians slaughter 800,000 other Rwandan Christians in ethnic genocide. Here was a country full of converts but with precious few disciples.

One could make a similar observation about other countries, like the United States, which, while thoroughly Christian in the early nineteenth century, also enslaved millions of human beings. Any country, any church, any group of Christians ignores God's call to holiness at its peril.

The teaching of James on works is often contrasted with that of the apostle Paul, but we forget that Paul also wrote:

If I have a faith that can move mountains, but do not have love, I am nothing. (1 Corinthians 13:2)

What shall we say, then? Shall we go on sinning so that grace may increase? By no means! We are those who have died to sin; how can we live in it any longer? . . . For we know that our old self was crucified with him so that the body ruled by sin might be done away with, that we should no longer be slaves to sin—because anyone who has died has been set free from sin. (Romans 6:1-2, 6-7)

The only thing that counts is faith expressing itself through love. (Galatians 5:6)

You, my brothers and sisters, were called to be free. But do not use your freedom to indulge the flesh; rather, serve one another humbly in love. For the entire law is fulfilled in keeping this one command: "Love your neighbor as yourself." If you bite and devour each other, watch out or you will be destroyed by each other. . . . The acts of the flesh are obvious: sexual immorality, impurity and debauchery; idolatry and witchcraft; hatred, discord, jealousy, fits of rage, selfish ambition, dissensions, factions and envy; drunkenness, orgies, and the like. I warn you, as I did before, that those who live like this will not inherit the kingdom of God. (Galatians 5:13-15, 19-21)

James could not agree more. Faith is never alone. While it is right, good and necessary that we spread the good news of God's free gift of salvation by grace through faith, if we do not give equal emphasis and training in godly living, in faith expressing itself in true love, we proclaim only half the gospel.

What's the main idea in this section?

What is one thing you can act on based on this reading?

[1]James R. Payton Jr., *Getting the Reformation Wrong* (Downers Grove, IL: InterVarsity Press, 2010), p. 122.
[2]Ibid., p. 123.

PART 4. DISCUSS
Putting It All Together

OPEN

What are some ways that we as Christians do not put actions behind our words?

READ JAMES 2:14-26.

"Easier said than done" is a cliché that certainly applies to Christian life. It is much easier to talk about God than to obey him. James said, "Even the demons believe there is one God." But that certainly does not make them Christians! That's why people can have all their doctrine perfectly straight and still miss out on God's will. James helps us to stay on target—to see how what we believe needs to be matched by the way we live.

1. James gives three examples that demonstrate the point that faith without works is dead. The first concerns care for the poor. Paraphrase this first example.

2. In part two, "Connect: Scripture to Scripture," we saw several of the many Old Testament passages that connect faith and spiritual activity with works. Look again at Isaiah 58:6-9. According to this passage, what does God desire?

3. What does it look like to do those things today—to care for the poor, set the oppressed free or loose the chains of injustice?

4. What blessings does God offer in the passage from Isaiah 58 to those who do what he desires?

5. What blessings have you experienced from doing what God desires?

6. In "Connect: Scripture to Scripture" we considered Matthew 22:37-39, where Jesus gives the two Great Commandments: "Love the Lord your God with all your heart and with all your soul and with all your mind" and "Love your neighbor as yourself." Based on the second of these commandments, how would you evaluate your love for God?

7. James refers to the story from Abraham's life when he took his son Isaac to be sacrificed in obedience to God. How does this story serve as a model for James's exhortations that faith must be accompanied by works?

8. Describe a time in your life or in the life of someone you know when obedience to God was or could have been at great personal cost.

9. Look at the account of Rahab in Joshua 2 and 6:15-25. What new details did you notice or were you struck by as you looked at her story?

10. How does Rahab demonstrate her faith by her works?

11. How does James show that God is not a respecter of persons, does not show favoritism, by comparing and contrasting Rahab and Abraham?

12. As we considered in "Reflect: Faith Is Never Alone," James is often wrongly considered to have preached a gospel of works alone in contrast to Paul, who is considered to have preached a gospel of faith alone. What do you learn about Paul's view of "works and faith" from portions of his letters in 1 Corinthians 13:2; Galatians 5:6, 13-15, 19-21; and Romans 6:1-2, 6-7?

13. How would you like to grow as a person of faith demonstrated by your works?

Ask God to help you follow through with the works that will reveal your true faith.

ON PREVENTING FOREST FIRES

James 3:1-12

WHERE WE'RE GOING

As mentioned in session two, after the introduction to the letter we find in James 1:19 what some see as a virtual table of contents for the rest of the book: "My dear brothers and sisters, take note of this: Everyone should be quick to listen, slow to speak and slow to become angry."

In James 1:22–2:26 he focused on the first of these three sections—being quick to hear. We learned that we should have our minds and hearts open to hear the Word of God. But hearing, in the Old Testament sense, is not just active listening. It's also doing. It is taking God's Word seriously enough that we put it into action.

Now, in James 3, he shifts his attention to the second part of James 1:19—being slow to speak. He especially has teachers in mind, as he sets out his theme in 3:1-2: "Not many of you should become teachers, my fellow believers, because you know that we who teach will be judged more strictly. We all stumble in many ways. Anyone who is never at fault in what they say is perfect, able to keep their whole body in check."

The opportunities for hypocrisy increase geometrically for those who teach. Outrage erupts routinely in the press and among common citizens when public figures don't live up to their own words and promises. A politician who breaks the public trust by helping himself to government funds. A firefighter who is guilty of arson. A preacher known for speaking far and wide against immorality who is caught with a prostitute. Just as James says, they are judged even more harshly than others who engage in the same wrongdoing.

As always, James pulls no punches. He goes right for the jugular. So if you are a teacher, you better fasten your seatbelt before you read James 3. It's going to be a bumpy ride.

Part 1. Investigate: James 3:1-12 (On Your Own)

Part 2. Connect: Scripture to Scripture (On Your Own)

Part 3. Reflect: The Trouble with Teachers (On Your Own)

Part 4. Discuss: Putting It All Together (With a Group)

A PRAYER TO PRAY

Lord and Father, how majestic is your name in all the earth. You made all of the magnificent creation—water, sky and land; fish, birds and animals. Yet you crowned humanity with glory and honor. We are, incredibly, made in your very image. While we have been given the responsibility to care and rule over creation, however, we cannot even rule over ourselves. As a result, we defame you with our unruly words when we attack other people made in your image. Our words, then, are very important. This is especially so for those of us who are teachers. We ask by your grace and mercy to guard our mouths—and to guard our hearts from which words of both cursing and blessing may come. May we speak your love and truth to the community of your people so that your name might be honored and your will be done. Amen.

PART 1. INVESTIGATE
James 3:1-12

Read James 3:1-12.

1. List the analogies and comparisons that James uses in these verses to describe the tongue.

2. The author suggests that not many people should become teachers (v. 1). What examples come to your mind of religious leaders or teachers whose lives people have judged more strictly than others?

   Why were they judged in this way?

3. Explain how the tongue has such control over our lives that a bit and a rudder are good comparisons (vv. 3-4).

4. What is the point of comparing the tongue to a fire and to a world of evil (vv. 5-6)?

5. Why is it so difficult to control the tongue (vv. 7-8)?

6. In what ways can the tongue poison people and relationships?

3:1. *Jewish sages also warned against teaching error and recognized that teachers would be judged strictly for leading others astray. Some who wanted to be teachers of wisdom were teaching the sort of "wisdom" espoused by the Jewish revolutionaries, which led to violence.*

3:7-8. *Although other creatures could be subdued as God commanded (Gen 1:28; 9:2), the tongue was like the deadliest snake, full of toxic venom (Ps 140:3; cf. 58:1-6, the Dead Sea Scrolls and other Jewish texts). Stoic philosophers also occasionally reflected on humanity's rule over animals.*

7. How do the analogies from nature (springs, trees, vines) highlight the inconsistencies of the tongue?

3:11-12. *James produces two other common examples of impossible incongruity. Figs, olives and grapes were the three most common agricultural products of the Judean hills, and alongside wheat they would have constituted the most common crops of the Mediterranean region as a whole. That everything brought forth after its kind was a matter of common observation and became proverbial in Greco-Roman circles (cf. also Gen 1:11-12, 21, 24-25).*

8. What inconsistencies do you see in the way you use your tongue?

9. James has focused primarily on the destructive power of the tongue. In what ways can the tongue also bring refreshment and healing?

10. What in this text gives you added strength and motivation to be more careful with your words?

11. What can you do to give God more praise? Be specific.

12. How can you give more affirmation to those you come in contact with each day?

Ask God to make your tongue a source of life rather than a source of destruction.

PART 2. CONNECT
Scripture to Scripture

NOT MANY SHOULD BECOME TEACHERS

Teachers were accorded high status in ancient Israel as well as in the early church. This could create some significant problems. Some of Jesus' most biting words were for the Pharisees and teachers of the law. In Matthew 23:13-36 Jesus offers seven piercing "woes" to these groups for their hypocrisy and the damage their teaching causes to others. James follows these themes from his Lord and master with his own strong admonitions.

We also see the link between James and Jesus in Matthew 7:1-2 and 12:34-37. According to these passages, why do teachers need to be especially cautious about what they say?

_____

_____

_____

_____

In James 3, we read that few should become teachers. In Matthew 23:5-8, Jesus says we aren't to be called teachers at all. Both James and Jesus signal by their statements the dangers of positions of authority. What complaints does Jesus have about the Pharisees and teachers of the law?

_____

_____

_____

_____

Have you been or wanted to be a teacher of the Bible or of how to live as a Christian? If so, from these passages, what should characterize your teaching?

_____

_____

_____

_____

WE ALL STUMBLE

When James says "We all stumble," he is sounding a theme found already in 1:26: "Those who consider themselves religious and yet do not keep a tight rein on their tongues deceive themselves, and their religion is worthless." He also draws on a familiar Old Testament notion. Paraphrase what each of these passages says about "stumbling" (being at fault).

Psalm 19:12-13:

_____

_____

Proverbs 20:7-9:

_____

_____

Jeremiah 17:9-10:

_____

_____

Ecclesiastes 7:19-20:

_____

_____

The above passages do not claim that we are hopelessly doomed to always sin. No. What hope do the following passages offer, just like James in 3:2?

Proverbs 13:3:

_____

_____

Proverbs 18:21:

_____

_____

In Matthew 5:21-22, how does Jesus raise the bar for upright behavior, especially regarding what we say?

_____

_____

_____

_____

BITS IN THE MOUTHS OF HORSES
In James 3:3-6 we find three mini-parables or analogies to the tongue and the whole body—the bit

and the horse, the rudder and the ship, and the spark and the fire. In each case, something very small can have a great effect. When we look back into Israel's ancient writings, we find other overtones at work in these three images. Fill in the table to see what Scripture says about horses.

	What is said about horses?	What is contrasted?
Psalm 20:7		
Psalm 33:16-19		
Psalm 147:10-11		
Proverbs 21:31		

What do horses represent in these passages?

_____

_____

_____

_____

The war horses of enemy armies can also represent God's judgment on his disobedient people. In Jeremiah 8:14-17 we read of the fear that such military might could induce. Likewise, Habakkuk 1:6-9 paints a fearful picture of an invincible cavalry galloping across the desert to bring destruction.

God's power over military might and masses of mounted soldiers is seen most clearly when Pharaoh's horsemen and chariots pursued the Israelites to the shores of the Red Sea. In Exodus 14:19-28 we read how God saved Israel from Egypt's army. And the song of praise to God in Exodus 15 begins by emphasizing his power to overwhelm Pharaoh's army of horses and men.

If God can rule over enemy cavalries, how much more can he do in our lives? Psalm 32 offers a higher goal than merely having a perfectly controlled tongue. How does the psalmist use the image of horses in verses 8-9 to convey what else God desires in us?

_____

_____

_____

_____

SHIPS AS AN EXAMPLE

James has already used the image of a ship in a storm in verse 1:6, where he wrote, "But when you ask, you must believe and not doubt, because the one who doubts is like a wave of the sea, blown and tossed by the wind." Now he adds a different dimension. Even though waves and wind toss a boat around, a pilot can use a rudder to guide the ship so it is not at the mercy of the sea. Likewise, when we begin to let God guide our words, we don't have to be at the mercy of our anger, jealousy or insecurity.

God has a perspective on ships and their activities. In Isaiah 2:12, 16-17, what do ships represent, and how does God respond?

_____

_____

_____

_____

Ships, just like today, were one of the most significant ways of conducting commerce in Old Testament times. Valuable goods were transported from place to place in a day when good roads were rare. Merchants made fortunes and nations gained power as a result. Yet God's people are not to rely on wealth or successful commerce, because they can make us proud and arrogant. In contrast to ships and the riches they bring, as Isaiah says, we should trust in the Lord. At God's hand our seemingly rock-solid wealth can come crashing down, humbling us in the process.

Read Psalm 107:23-32. When tossed by a storm, how do people respond, and what is the Lord's reaction?

_____

_____

_____

_____

When James talks about a rudder guiding a ship, he also calls to mind the virtue of humility and trusting God. We all stumble and have trouble controlling our words. But instead of trying to run our lives and our words by our own efforts, we can make the Lord our captain. If we allow him to be the pilot who controls the rudder of our words, we can also rely on him for all that we do and are.

With the image of horses, James brings to mind military might. With ships, economic wealth. With both come arrogance and pride which lead to imprudent, harsh and cruel words. In your own experience or in world events you've observed, how have power and wealth led to destructive words and actions?

_____

_____

_____

_____

GREAT BOASTS

Like a bit and a rudder, "the tongue is a small part of the body, but it makes great boasts" (3:5). Let's consider the tradition of the Psalms and the Prophets that James draws on to gain more insight.

In the Psalms, boasting isn't about telling people how many A's you got on tests or how many sports trophies your son won or the size of your prize-winning tomatoes. Something much more serious is in mind. For each of the following passages, list the verbs used to describe what people do with their mouths that displeases God.

Psalm 12:1-5: _____

Psalm 52:1-4: _____

Psalm 73:1-10: _____

Now, looking at the same passages, list the kinds of physical action and violence their words lead to.

Psalm 12:1-5: _____

Psalm 52:1-4: _____

Psalm 73:1-10: _____

We say, "Sticks and stones may break our bones, but words will never hurt us." But for the psalmists, words are just the first step to violence. Words are used to plunder the poor and place burdens on the needy. Words are used to plot ways to destroy people and threaten those who are weak.

Does James have physical violence in mind when he mentions the problems words can cause? As we have seen, concern for the poor and oppressed ("widows and orphans") has been an emphasis all through his letter. The Psalms give us a clue. It is no accident that closely connected to a "boastful tongue" in Psalm 12 is the Lord's response that "because the poor are plundered and the needy groan, I will now arise." It is the arrogance of the rich and powerful that leads their tongues to plot destruction (Psalm 52:2) and threaten oppression (Psalm 73:8).

Sometimes the violence of the rich against the poor is obvious—in countries where warfare causes the starvation of thousands or even millions, for example. But there may be other situations where it is less apparent because of the lack of a crisis. Large populations may remain in grinding poverty for decades or even generations while some in the same country enjoy great wealth. It is the power of words (whether in the law of the land or the threats of the strong) that can cause these conditions to remain unchanged for years.

James's words about boasting and the tongue may seem strong. But in this context we can see why James would say, "The tongue also is a fire, a world of evil among the parts of the body. It corrupts the whole body, sets the whole course of one's life on fire, and is itself set on fire by hell" (3:6).

There is a kind of boasting, however, that pleases God. Read Jeremiah 9:23-24 and fill in the table to see what kind it is.

Who Should Not Boast	What They Should Not Boast In	Instead They Should Boast That They Understand God, Who Exercises ...

How can your life be aligned with the right-hand side?

_____

_____

_____

_____

THE TONGUE IS A FIRE

Fire was a necessity of life for warmth and food in the ancient world. In Scripture fire is used to communicate a range of meanings. It represents the presence of God for worship (the burning bush in Exodus 3:2), for guidance or protection (the pillar of fire in Exodus 13:21), for purification (Isaiah 6:6-7; Jeremiah 6:29) or for destruction (Sodom and Gomorrah in Genesis 19:24). It burns up sacrifices (e.g., Leviticus 2:2). And it can be an instrument of warfare (e.g., against Jericho in Joshua 6:24 and Jerusalem in Judges 1:8). Obviously James has destructive effects in mind.[1]

Proverbs makes an explicit connection between words and fire. Read Proverbs 16:27-30. Like fire, what kind of far-reaching destructive effects can words have?

_____

_____

_____

_____

Now look at Proverbs 26:20-22. How is gossip like fire?

_____

_____

How would you define gossip?

_____

_____

_____

Why do we like to share gossip with others so much? What is so appealing to us about doing it?

_____

_____

_____

_____

How can you guard yourself against gossip?

_____

_____

_____

_____

James also builds on Jesus' teaching about the destructive force of words. In Matthew 15:10-11, 17-20 he shows us another reason why we need to be aware of what we say. What do our words reveal?

_____

_____

_____

What happens when these words are put into action?

_____

_____

_____

_____

Just as a fire can raze an entire forest, so words can devastate a whole community.

CORRUPTING THE WHOLE BODY

James says the tongue "corrupts the whole body." What we say affects our whole person, for good or ill. If we regularly have bitter or angry words for other people, we will be bitter or angry people. If our words are commonly encouraging and affirming, that marks our whole life and personality as well.

In the New Testament Paul is also known for using the word *body* as a metaphor for the community of believers gathered in Christ. Look up these verses from Paul's letter to the Ephesians: 1:22-23; 2:11-16; and 4:16.

What do we learn about Christ and the church?

_____

_____

_____

_____

In Ephesians 2:14-16 especially, Paul emphasizes that the body of Christ is to be a place of reconciliation, peace and unity. Even the divisions between Gentiles and Jews that had been brewing for centuries were to be ended as all found oneness in Christ.

Now consider 1 Corinthians 12:25-27. How is this similar to what James explains in 3:6 about the body?

_____

_____

_____

_____

As James says in 3:1, the focus of his attention in this chapter is on teachers. Unlike the rest of us, they have a special burden, because what they say affects the whole community. While our words may affect three, six or ten people (and that is definitely something to be taken seriously), what a teacher says affects the whole church. Teachers who are always critical of others (whether those in the church or not) can change the whole personality of a church to be divisive. When this comes to fruition, it can tear a church apart from the inside or destructively set groups of Christians against one another. Christ, however, came to heal divisions and reconcile all to himself.

If you are a teacher, James has his attention focused on you. What should teachers do to make sure their words do not foster anger, division or criticism within the body of Christ?

_____

_____

_____

_____

SET ON FIRE BY HELL

The Greek word translated "hell" in James 3:6 is *Gehenna*, the name for a valley just to the south of Jerusalem. This valley (in Hebrew, the Valley of *Hinnom*) was the boundary between the tribes of Judah and Benjamin (see Joshua 15:8). But it had a darker history as well.

Read 2 Kings 23:8-10 and Jeremiah 7:30-31. What violence was committed in the Valley of Hinnom?

_____

_____

_____

_____

In New Testament times the valley was used as a garbage dump where refuse was constantly burned. Jesus referenced the valley as a picture of the punishment that awaits those who are separated from God, such as in Matthew 5:30.

Just before that in the Sermon on the Mount, Jesus also used the word *Gehenna*. How is what Jesus says in Matthew 5:22 similar to James's thought in 3:6?

_____

_____

_____

_____

How should Jesus' and James's words affect the way we speak of or to other Christians we disagree with about major or minor matters?

_____

_____

_____

_____

ALL KINDS ARE TAMED

Genesis 1:20-28, Psalm 8:3-9 and James 3 concur about humanity ruling over (taming) all living creatures. What irony does James point out, however, in verse 7-8?

_____

_____

_____

In James 3:8, an untamed tongue is said to be full of deadly poison. Psalm 140:1-5 illustrates James's point well when it uses the image of poison. But it's not just the poisonous words of evildoers the psalmist fears. What else concerns him?

_____

_____

_____

_____

PRAISING AND CURSING

In 3:9-10, James considers a further irony—praising and cursing can both come out of the same mouth. Here he continues drawing themes from Genesis 1, in this case particularly from Genesis 1:27: "So God created mankind in his own image, in the image of God he created them; male and female he created them." How does James reason that cursing people is essentially equivalent to cursing God?

_____

_____

_____

_____

The theological point James is making about all people being made in God's image builds on his injunction in chapter 2 to not show favoritism. A person is not more valuable in God's sight for being rich or poor. All should be treated with courtesy and honor.

In verse 10 James targets another outrageous irony. Here we are in church, praising God, while also speaking violently against others with the same mouth! How have you seen Christians treat each other badly over various disagreements in the church?

_____

_____

_____

_____

How could the situation have been handled differently so that everyone was treated as one made in the image of God?

_____

_____

_____

_____

In 3:11-12 James offers three more mini-parables to make his point. A saltwater spring can't produce fresh water. A fig tree can't bear olives. A grapevine can't bear figs. How do the last two, especially, also echo Genesis 1, rooting his teaching in creation itself?

_____

_____

_____

_____

We hear clear echoes of Jesus' teaching here in James as well—not just in the use of parables but even in the particular parables James chooses to illustrate his points. What parables does Jesus offer in Matthew 7:16-18 and 12:33-37?

_____

_____

_____

_____

What point of Jesus' in these passages from Matthew does James touch on in chapter 3?

_____

_____

_____

_____

Think of leaders in your Christian community. What are some things they are doing well?

_____

_____

_____

_____

_____

_____

Take a minute to write a note to one or two of these people, thanking them for what they've done.

[1]See "Fire," in Leland Ryken, James C. Wilhoit and Tremper Longman III, eds., *Dictionary of Biblical Imagery* (Downers Grove, IL: InterVarsity Press, 1998), pp. 286-89.

PART 3. REFLECT
The Trouble with Teachers

Richard, the pastor of a megachurch in Florida, had a widespread reputation as a powerful speaker and leader. Over a period of twenty years his church had grown to several thousand, and he enjoyed a high degree of influence among other church leaders and churchgoers around the country. He was also a sought-after conference speaker and successful author.

One year he was a member of the program planning committee for his denomination's next annual national convention. Also on the committee were a half dozen other pastors and denominational leaders from around the country. The first day the group met, they worked together well on a number of issues.

On the morning of the second day, however, Richard became very belligerent toward Donald, the chair of the committee. In fact, his anger ultimately boiled over into a tirade. Richard was incensed that Donald had not attended or graduated from one of the denomination's seminaries. What right did he have to lead this committee? He was clearly unqualified. If he had any sense of principle, he would resign as chair immediately.

The committee was stunned. Donald had been a pastor in good standing in the denomination for fifteen years. True, he had not attended a seminary specifically affiliated with their denomination, but he had been ordained according to the standards and practices of the denomination without any question then or since. In addition, Donald had been properly appointed chair of the planning committee by the denomination's leadership, of which Richard was not a member.

After Richard's fifteen-minute barrage, Donald, like the rest of the committee, was not sure how to respond. When Richard seemed to conclude, Donald made a few neutral comments and then suggested the group temporarily adjourn, which they did. Later the committee reconvened and somehow managed, awkwardly, to conclude their business without the issue coming up again.

In the days and weeks that followed, Donald began to ask for advice and get counsel from the other committee members and denominational leaders. What had happened? Donald knew Richard by reputation but did not know him personally, so he wasn't sure what to make of it all or what to do next.

What Donald began to find out was that this was not the first time Richard had acted in this way. In fact, Richard's outbursts in the middle of meetings were a common pattern, one not just of anger but also of attempting to assert control over others. By injecting an element of fear, Richard made sure group members would not think of earning his wrath by crossing him on other issues.

The result was a path of destruction left in Richard's wake. If someone didn't quite conform to his particular standards or agree with his ways of doing things (whether at his church or in the denomination), Richard would at some point turn his explosive anger on them. This would often lead to the person in question being demoted, fired or removed—if they didn't just leave voluntarily first.

Those who had been victims of Richard's anger were left feeling injured and often embittered. Some left the church altogether. Some wandered away from faith. Some managed to hold on and eventually find God's healing.

Many over the years benefited from Richard's ministry and leadership, of course. But others who remained and worked more closely with Richard sometimes suffered as well. Though they appreciated his vision and passion, they were on guard, and their contributions were stifled, knowing they could be Richard's next target.

What surprised Donald most, however, was discovering that in all the years Richard had been acting this way, no one had ever confronted him about his behavior. Richard was such a respected, influential and intimidating figure, even his seniors did not challenge him.

James, as a leader of the first-century church in Jerusalem, would not have hesitated to do so, however. As he writes, "Consider what a great forest is set on fire by a small spark. The tongue also is a fire, a world of evil among the parts of the body. It corrupts the whole body, sets the whole course of one's life on fire, and is itself set on fire by hell" (3:5-6).

You wouldn't have to be the pastor of a megachurch to receive James's rebuke. You could be the pastor or an elder in a congregation of a hundred, the Sunday school teacher of ten, or the committee head of five. Too often churches are peppered with leaders who act as if their authority should be unquestioned, forcing their choices on others. As James suggested in chapter 2, sometimes people who have no formal positions of leadership but who are major donors to a church or organization think their money gives them special privileges and therefore act in rude, high-handed or manipulative ways.

Such behavior from leaders is sometimes salted with harsh, angry, manipulative comments and destructive behavior that burn individuals and the church as a whole. But there is no place in Christ's body for un-Christlike behavior, no matter what the issue—whether doctrine or styles of worship or the latest hot debate to inflict the church.

Once two of the twelve apostles, James (probably not the James who wrote this letter) and John, asked Jesus if they could sit at his right and left hand in his kingdom—the two positions of the highest prestige and power. The other ten were indignant with the two.

Jesus told them all, "You know that those who are regarded as rulers of the Gentiles lord it over them, and their high officials exercise authority over them. Not so with you. Instead, whoever wants to become great among you must be your servant, and whoever wants to be first must be slave of all. For even the Son of Man did not come to be served, but to serve, and to give his life as a ransom for many" (Mark 10:42-45).

Pastors, deacons and elders in churches sometimes think they should be making all the decisions, that they don't need to consult with others, that there is no need for by-laws (or, if they exist, that such by-laws can be ignored). This is the exact opposite of what Jesus and James call for. The role of the leader is to serve, not to be served by accumulating honor, respect, privilege, money or power.

In James's view, teachers are especially out of line when they criticize, rebuke and insult those they disagree with. Their tongues corrupt the whole body of Christ; Christians start using power plays to remove people from positions of responsibility, or churches become contentious and divided. Instead of being blessed peacemakers, teachers become peacebreakers who are to be rejected.

Every teacher, pastor and Christian leader should seriously and honestly ask themselves these questions:

- As I look over my time in ministry, what conflicts have I been involved with? (List each one and when it occurred, and then write several paragraphs summarizing what happened in each case.)

- What patterns of conflict with others do I see here—causes, personalities, roles of people involved, situations, time of year, etc.?

- When there was conflict, when was there reconciliation? When were relationships broken? Is there a pattern here, and if so what characterizes it?

- When have I been a peacemaker for others who were in conflict with each other?

- Who am I under the authority of—real authority, not just in name or title?

- Is there someone who is honest with me about my faults and failings? If so, who? If not, why not? (Also, if not, make a list of possible people who could play this role in your life. Then form a plan to approach someone about meeting with you regularly to give you straightforward input about your life and ministry.)

It would be worthwhile to take half a day or a full day to deliberately journal through and pray through these questions. Then take those responses to someone who is not under your authority, someone you trust and who will keep confidence, someone who will not be intimidated by you, and someone to whom you give permission to be absolutely honest with you. (While this exercise is especially needed for leaders and teachers, it is, of course, valuable for any Christian.)

After several months of counsel from other leaders as well as his own meditation and prayer, Donald made an appointment to meet with Richard to discuss the committee. Richard was in another state at the time, and getting together with members between their committee meetings was not required. Yet Donald felt this was right and necessary.

First they talked about things of common interest and then some neutral points of business. Then Donald carefully, quietly and clearly expressed to Richard how his comments and the way he expressed them at the previous committee meeting were inappropriate, as they were not in the spirit of what the denomination valued, of the rules that governed disputes or of common Christian courtesy. After a moment of reflection, Richard asked if Donald wanted him to resign from the committee. Donald said that was not his intent. His goal was reconciliation and moving forward positively.

Richard did stay on the committee. Was there complete reconciliation? Was Richard totally reformed after this encounter? Did he become a new man and change his ways? Because this was the real world, because people are messy and because Richard had a lifelong pattern of behavior which had become a character trait, it would be saying too much to claim that this one encounter made everything new and right. But it was a step in putting out a fire.

What's the main idea in this section?

What is one thing you can act on based on this reading?

PART 4. DISCUSS
Putting It All Together

OPEN

How have you seen destructive words damage in the news or in the lives of people you know?

READ JAMES 3:1-12.

One of the most distressing crises is a fire out of control. The pain of seeing the resulting destruction can be devastating. Personal belongings going up in smoke. The beauty of nature marred. Even the loss of life itself. Hurtful words can have much the same impact.

1. James says in verse 1 that teachers are judged more strictly. What examples can you think of where others were judged more strictly because of their position?

2. In James 3:3-6 we find three mini-parables or analogies to the tongue and the whole body: the bit and the horse, the rudder and the ship, and the spark and the fire. In each case, something very small has a great effect. Habakkuk 1:8 paints a fearful picture of an invincible cavalry galloping across the desert to bring destruction. Why would James compare the tongue to a bit in a horse's mouth?

3. As you consider the huge task of controlling your tongue, what hope does it give you to know that God rules over mighty war horses?

4. Using the analogy of a rudder that controls a ship, what would the effect on your wordsw—and, in turn, your actions, thoughts and perspective—be if the Lord were the captain of the ship?

5. Fires started by one small spark can do devastating damage. In what ways can the tongue be equally destructive?

6. Why is fire a good metaphor for gossip?

7. Why is gossip tempting?

8. How can you guard yourself from gossip?

9. James uses extremely serious terms when he speaks of the tongue and the damage it can do. Jesus also uses extreme language when talking about words in Matthew 5:21-22 and 15:33-37. Based on both passages in Matthew, what would you say James means when he says that the tongue corrupts the whole person, sets the course of his life on fire and is set on fire by hell itself?

10. How have you seen both blessing and cursing coming out of your mouth?

11. Why is it so serious to "curse men"?

12. What specific things can you do to praise God more? To affirm instead of criticizing others?

13. James 3:2 says, "If anyone is never at fault in what he says, he is a perfect person, able to keep the whole body in check." We are not perfect. We do stumble. But as followers of Jesus our goal is to keep our words in check for his glory. In part three there is a list of questions for you to reflect on which could help you evaluate your patterns of communication. Review that list now and share from it some of what you discovered about the ways you tend to communicate.

Bring to the Lord the ways you have been hurt by painful words. Confess to the Lord how you have hurt others with your words. Ask him to reveal any damage that you have done with words that you do not know about.

MAKERS AND BREAKERS OF PEACE

James 3:13–4:10

WHERE WE'RE GOING

Trying to outline the letter of James can feel like trying to nail jelly to the wall. Just when you think you have it figured out, it keeps moving. Obviously, James has several themes that keep popping in and out—wisdom, rich and poor, doing the Word not just listening to it, watching what we say, and more.

In this session we see the conclusion of one section at the end of James 3 (on not using destructive words) seamlessly transitioning into another at the beginning of James 4 (on not engaging in angry disputes). All these themes build on and interweave with each other. If we are quick to hear we must by definition also be slow to speak. And if we are slow to jump in and speak our mind about God's Word, that will reduce the chances of becoming angry in God's name.

So, with confidence that God will be with us as we continue our journey into James (but also with some legitimate trepidation), we move forward in this striking letter to God's people.

Part 1. Investigate: James 3:13–4:10 (On Your Own)

Part 2. Connect: Scripture to Scripture (On Your Own)

Part 3. Reflect: Peacemakers Who Sow in Peace
(On Your Own)

Part 4. Discuss: Putting It All Together (With a Group)

A PRAYER TO PRAY

Our Lord, we know that you are pure, peace-loving, impartial and full of mercy. Yet we also know that you oppose the proud and boast-

ful, the envious, those who are full of selfish ambition. Grant us the grace to draw near to you, to resist the devil, and to confess and mourn over our sins so that your wisdom from above might envelope both your people and our own hearts, and that we might reap a harvest of righteousness. Amen.

PART 1. INVESTIGATE
James 3:13–4:10

Read James 3:13–4:10.

1. Who is this section addressed to (see 3:13)?

2. How is this similar to 3:1?

3. In 3:13-18 James discusses earthly and heavenly wisdom. What are the characteristics of each?

4. When have you seen the kind of wisdom that comes from heaven help resolve conflict (3:18)?

5. What would you say is the difference between James's description in 3:17 and being a doormat?

6. What does James say is the source of quarrels (4:1-2)?

7. In contrast, James says we should deal with our desires by asking God for what we want (4:2-3). Why do we sometimes resist or hesitate to ask God for what we want?

3:14. *The term translated "jealousy" (NASB) or "envy" (NIV, NRSV) here is the term for "zeal" used by the Zealots, who fancied themselves successors of Phinehas (Num 25:11; Ps 106:30-31) and the Maccabees and sought to liberate Jewish Palestine from Rome by force of arms. "Strife" (KJV; "selfish ambition"—NASB, NIV, NRSV) also was related to disharmony and had been known to provoke wars.*

3:15-16. *"Above" was sometimes synonymous with "God" in Jewish tradition; as opposed to heavenly wisdom, the wisdom of violence (3:14) was thoroughly earthly, human and demonic (cf. similarly Mt 16:22-23). The Dead Sea Scrolls spoke of sins as inspired by the spirit of error, and folk Judaism believed that people were continually surrounded by hordes of demons. James's words suggest a more indirect working of demons through stirring up their own ungodly values in the world system.*

8. James says we don't receive even when we ask with wrong motives (4:3). What might be some examples of right and wrong motives in prayer?

9. What does it mean for us to have "friendship with the world" (4:4)?

10. Besides pure motives, what else does James say is necessary in order to come to God in prayer (4:4-10)?

11. How do each of these contribute to a humble spirit?

12. James sounds harsh here. Do you think he is being extreme or is he on target? Explain.

13. Are there situations where humility could help you become a source of peace this coming week? Explain.

4:2. *Diatribe often included hyperbole, or graphic, rhetorical exaggeration for effect. Most of James's readers have presumably not literally killed anyone, but they are exposed to violent teachers (3:13-18) who regard murder as a satisfactory means of attaining justice.*

4:7 *Ancient magical texts spoke of demons' fleeing before incantations, but the idea here is moral, not magical. One must choose between the values of God and those of the world (4:4), between God's wisdom and that which is demonic (3:15, 17). The point is that a person who lives by God's values (in this case, his way of peace) is no part of Satan's kingdom (in contrast to the religious-sounding revolutionaries).*

Take a few minutes to be quiet in God's presence. Ask God to help you become a peacemaker during the coming week and to show you how this might happen.

PART 2. CONNECT
Scripture to Scripture

James 3:1 began a section addressing teachers; 3:13 indicates he is continuing to address this group, "the wise and understanding among you."

WISE AND UNDERSTANDING

James picks up the phrase "wise and understanding among you" from the beginning of the book of Deuteronomy. There, in Deuteronomy 1:9-18, Moses reviews for Israel how years before he had organized the nation and set leaders over them to help him when they were first in the wilderness, after they crossed the Red Sea and escaped from Egypt. Note the different aspects mentioned of the "wise and understanding" in Deuteronomy 1:9-18.

Where They Are to Be Chosen From	How They Are to Be Organized	How They Are to Conduct Their Duties

What similarities do you see here between what Moses says and what James has been saying not only in chapter 3 but throughout his letter?

_____

_____

_____

_____

Back in session one when we first looked at the theme of wisdom, we considered Isaiah 11:1-3, where the prophet also pairs wisdom and understanding, speaking of "the Spirit of wisdom and of understanding" that will rest on the Messiah who is to come and rule. Jesus, of course, is the model of this kind of leadership we are all to emulate.

James yet again reveals the strong influence of his Master, Jesus. In Matthew 11:18-19, Jesus says that the Pharisees are never satisfied, no matter what they see in other teachers outside their group. What similarities do you see between James 3:13 and what Jesus says in Matthew 11:18-19?

_____

_____

_____

_____

Just a few verses later, in Matthew 11:28-30, we find another theme picked up in James 3:13. Express in your own words how the kind of leadership Jesus exemplifies differs from what James is complaining about.

_____

_____

_____

Think about areas of responsibility you have—at church, in your family, at work, in school, with friends, in your community. How can you show evidence of your wisdom by fulfilling those tasks the way Jesus does and the way James recommends?

_____

_____

_____

THE THREEFOLD DESCRIPTION OF "WISDOM" FROM BELOW

In James 3:15 we find what characterizes the wisdom that James euphemistically says "does not come down from heaven." What are the three traits of such "wisdom"?

1. _____

2. _____

3. _____

The number three is a symbol of completeness. Elijah doused the wood on the altar at Mt. Carmel three times to emphasize that it was thoroughly soaked (1 Kings 18:30-35). Jesus likewise came to ask the disciples to stay awake and pray with him three times in Gethsemane, emphasizing the completeness of their failure (Matthew 26:36-47). James's threefold description of the "wisdom" of bitter envy and selfish ambition also underscores how entirely corrupt that kind of "wisdom" is.

Why is it so easy to confuse our own ambitions with our ambition for God's work and purposes?

_____

_____

_____

What are some things you can do to avoid this pitfall?

_____

_____

_____

THE SEVENFOLD DESCRIPTION OF WISDOM FROM ABOVE

List the contrasting sevenfold description of wisdom from heaven found in James 3:17.

1. _____   5. full of _____ and _____

2. _____   6. _____

3. _____   7. _____

4. _____

Seven is also a number that symbolizes perfection or completeness in the Bible. In Genesis 2:1-3 God rested from the work of creation on the seventh day, emphasizing the completeness of his labor. And many of the Old Testament rituals involved the number seven—for example, the sprinkling of blood (Leviticus 4:6), burnt offerings (Numbers 28:11), the Feast of Unleavened Bread and the Feast of Tabernacles (Exodus 12:15, 19), and praise to God described by one of the psalmists (Psalm 119:164).

James named the topic of this section in 3:13—wisdom that shows itself in good deeds and humility. As we saw in session one, wisdom is not just being smart or clever or highly educated. (There's nothing wrong with these, of course; they just aren't what the Bible means by wisdom.) Rather, wisdom is knowing God's will and doing it. So let's examine how these seven characteristics show themselves in good deeds and humiilty.

Pure. The first characteristic of wisdom from above is being pure. Look at each of these passages and fill in what you find.

	What is said about purity?	What is contrasted as impure in each passage?
Psalm 12:5-6		
Psalm 73:12-19		
Isaiah 1:15-17		

What then do these passages suggest are the "pure" good deeds that are the fruit of wisdom?

_____

_____

_____

_____

Peaceable. The second characteristic of wisdom from above is being peaceable. In English the word means, at its most basic, the absence of war or fighting. But the Hebrew word, *shalom*, which stood behind James's Greek equivalent (*eirene*, from which we get our English word *irenic*), has a much broader and deeper significance. The word *shalom* is not always translated as "peace" in English Bibles. Sometimes it is "prosperity" or "well-being" or "harmony" or simply "blessing." This helps give the range of meanings found in this complex word. It may also explain why, depending on your Bible translation, you won't necessarily find the word *peace* in each of the passages below.

Read the passages and list the other blessings from God that are associated with peace in each case.

Numbers 6:24-26: _____

Ezekiel 37:24-28: _____

Isaiah 9:6: _____

Psalm 85:8-13: _____

Proverbs 3:13-18: _____

From these words and passages, then, write your own definition of what *shalom* entails.

_____

_____

_____

_____

Considerate and submissive. When James lists being considerate or gentle as the third fruit of wisdom from above, he once again echoes themes found in the Sermon on the Mount, where Jesus says, "Blessed are the meek, for they will inherit the earth" (Matthew 5:5).

We also just looked (under the subheading "Wise and Understanding") at Matthew 11:28-30, where Jesus identifies himself as being meek and lowly. Later in Matthew (21:1-11), Jesus triumphantly enters Jerusalem the Sunday before his crucifixion, riding on a donkey. In verses 4-5 Matthew quotes Zechariah 9:9, explaining that Jesus has fulfilled the prophet's words: "Say to Daughter Zion, 'See, your king comes to you, gentle and riding on a donkey, and on a colt, the foal of a donkey.'"

What examples can you think of in which teachers or leaders acted toward others with consideration or gentleness?

_____

_____

_____

_____

_____

The NIV translates the fourth fruit of wisdom from above as being submissive. Other English translations call it being willing to yield, being reasonable or being open to reason. It's easy to see why this character trait would be associated with humility and contrasted with selfish ambition.

Full of mercy and good fruit. James uses a pair of terms to describe the fifth fruit of wisdom from above. Whereas teachers were warned not to let their tongues be "*full of* deadly poison" (3:8), here by contrast they are to be "*full of* mercy and good fruit." What does this mean? How are these two attributes connected?

_____

_____

_____ .

_____

Mercy received its most significant treatment earlier in James's letter in 2:12-13, which reads, "Speak and act as those who are going to be judged by the law that gives freedom, because judgment without mercy will be shown to anyone who has not been merciful. Mercy triumphs over judgment." This seems like the conclusion of a section, and it is. But it would be a mistake to think there is no connection to what immediately follows. Look at James 2:14-17. How is this mini-parable an example of mercy and good fruit?

_____

_____

_____

_____

Impartial and sincere. The sixth fruit, being impartial, has also received coverage in James. We need only go back to James 2:1-9 for a quick refresher. We can easily see why showing favoritism would create the disorder (3:16) and divisions he is fighting so hard to undo.

The seventh fruit is being sincere or (as some translations put it) being without hypocrisy. Jesus thundered against the Pharisees and teachers of the law in Matthew 23:1-36 with seven biting woes, calling them "you hypocrites." What we may forget, however, is that tucked into the middle of this denunciation is a call to humility and servanthood among his own disciples. In Matthew 23:11-12 he says, "The greatest among you will be your servant. For those who exalt themselves will be humbled, and those who humble themselves will be exalted."

How do Jesus' vision of leadership and James's sevenfold description of the fruit of wisdom from above stand in stark contrast to the common way people lead and teach in the church and in the world?

_____

_____

_____

SOW IN PEACE, REAP A HARVEST OF RIGHTEOUSNESS

We've already considered *shalom* as the second fruit of wisdom from above. Here in 3:18 James comes back to it, this time drawing on Old Testament imagery of the harvest. Fill in the table to see this more clearly.

	What the Righteous Receive	**What the Wicked Receive**
Proverbs 11:18		
Proverbs 11:19		
Proverbs 11:30-31		
Proverbs 13:2		
Isaiah 32:18-19		
Hosea 10:12-13		

James concludes this section by emphasizing the blessings peacemakers receive. Jesus concluded his Beatitudes in the Sermon on the Mount by also linking peacemaking and righteousness. "Blessed are the peacemakers, for they will be called children of God. Blessed are those who are persecuted because of righteousness, for theirs is the kingdom of heaven" (Matthew 5:9-10).

FIGHTS AND QUARRELS

James now moves to his third main theme: be slow to anger. Teachers can be destructive with their tongues if they do not follow the way of humility and servant leadership. As he says in 4:1, however, fights and quarrels can also erupt between various factions. James once again uses strong language to describe what he sees: "You desire but do not have, so you kill" (4:2).

Jesus did the same thing in the Sermon on the Mount: "You have heard that it was said to the people long ago, 'You shall not murder, and anyone who murders will be subject to judgment.' But I tell you that anyone who is angry with a brother or sister will be subject to judgment" (Matthew 5:21-22).

When have you been angry recently? No doubt there were external circumstances at work. And it is always easy to blame others. But instead, take a moment to reflect only on yourself. What was going on inside you at the time?

_____

_____

_____

_____

It is possible that James has more than verbal fights in mind. Scot McKnight writes, "Religious violence, anchored as it was in both Old Testament and ancient ways, was more common to that society [of James's day] than most of us care to admit, and a good example is Paul's own example (Acts 8:3; 9:1-2, 21; 22:4, 19; 26:10-11; Gal 1:23). Nor has the church failed to keep the pace with ancient violence—one needs to think of the bloody battles around Nicea, Constantine, the Crusades, the Reformation, the Inquisition and beyond."[1]

ASK AND RECEIVE

We have seen how often James draws on Jesus and the Sermon on the Mount in particular. Yet in 4:3 he seems to be saying something quite different from what Jesus says in Matthew 7:7-8. James writes, "When you ask, you do not receive, because you ask with wrong motives, that you may spend what you get on your pleasures," while Jesus teaches, "Ask and it will be given to you; seek and you will find; knock and the door will be opened to you. For everyone who asks receives; the one who seeks finds; and to the one who knocks, the door will be opened."

How do these passages actually go together?

_____

_____

_____

_____

Now consider James 1:5-6, "If any of you lacks wisdom, you should ask God, who gives generously to all without finding fault, and it will be given to you. But when you ask, you must believe and not doubt, because the one who doubts is like a wave of the sea, blown and tossed by the wind." What insight does this bring in putting these thoughts together?

YOU ADULTEROUS PEOPLE

The Old Testament, especially the prophets, often likens the nation of Israel to a bride—the bride of God, specifically, and all too often a bride who has been unfaithful to her husband, committing adultery, as it were, with false gods. As Jeremiah said, "'But like a woman unfaithful to her husband, so you, Israel, have been unfaithful to me,' declares the LORD" (Jeremiah 3:20). Jesus also used the same analogy for the Israel of his day (see Matthew 12:39; 16:4).

One of the most remarkable undertakings God gave any of the prophets was to Hosea. Read Hosea 1:2-3. What does God call him to do and why?

_____

_____

_____

_____

Later Hosea's wife Gomer leaves him and ends up under the control of another man. Read Hosea 3:1-5. What does God now call Hosea to do and why?

_____

_____

_____

_____

Clearly, calling God's people "adulterers" is strong language. But what hope is offered in Hosea even in circumstances as desolate as Israel's?

_____

_____

_____

_____

So when James says in 4:5 that God "jealously longs for the spirit he has caused to dwell in us," James is echoing the thought in Exodus 34:14, "Do not worship any other god, for the LORD, whose name is Jealous, is a jealous God." It is not inappropriate for a husband to be jealous if another man is pursuing his wife. God will not stand by impassively if someone is trying to steal his people. He will actively work to bring them back to him. If he weren't jealous in this way, it would mean he didn't actually love us. So we can take comfort that God shows how much he cares about us by coming after us even when we are pulled away.

THE PROUD AND THE HUMBLE
Rather than offering an Old Testament allusion, in verse 4:6 James directly quotes Proverbs 3:34. As is often the case in Proverbs, we find in 3:32-35 a number of stark contrasts. List them.

	Who God Opposes	How God Opposes Them	Who God Favors	How God Favors Them
3:32				
3:33				
3:34				
3:35				

SUBMIT TO GOD, RESIST THE DEVIL
In James 4:7 we read, "Submit yourselves, then, to God. Resist the devil, and he will flee from you." Read Matthew 4:1-11. In this passage, what temptations did Jesus face?

_____

_____

_____

_____

List the ways Jesus submitted to God here.

_____

_____

_____

_____

List the ways he resisted the devil.

_____

_____

_____

_____

What can you learn from this as you face the temptation to get angry with those you disagree with or are tempted to be in conflict with others?

_____

_____

_____

_____

COMING NEAR TO GOD

When James says, "Come near to God and he will come near to you" (4:8), he is not giving an absolute cause and effect. In other words, he's not suggesting that God only comes near if we make the first move toward God. Rather, he is showing that we have a real part to play in our relationship with God. We are not puppets or robots. We are people whose decisions matter. And how we decide to relate to God makes a difference.

See how this theme is presented in the Old Testament. Draw a line connecting each Scripture passage with the idea(s) it expresses. (Note: Some Scripture passages may have two phrases associated with them. And sometimes two passages may connect to a single phrase. Make sure every passage and idea have at least one connection.)

Deuteronomy 4:7	God came near when I called.
2 Chronicles 15:2	The Lord is near to those who call on him.
Malachi 3:7	If we seek God, we will find him.
Psalm 145:18	Return to God, and he will return to you.
Lamentations 3:57	God is near when we pray to him.
Zechariah 1:2-3	If we forsake God, he will forsake us.

These Old Testament passages use similar but slightly different phrases. In your own words describe the slightly different meaning of each or what might be involved in each phrase:

"Calling on God" means _____

"Seeking God" means _____

"Returning to God" means _____

Which of these resonates most deeply with you and why?

_____

_____

_____

_____

WASH AND PURIFY

Washing or cleansing is how the people of Israel in the Old Testament were purified or consecrated to the Lord. This could involve washing clothes and bathing (Exodus 19:10; Leviticus 17:15-16) or removing things that were in themselves considered unclean, like certain kinds of animals (2 Chronicles 29:4-5, 15-16). The purpose of washing was to be cleansed from guilt and sin (Job 9:28-30; Psalm 51:2).[2]

Note at least three similar ideas found in Psalm 24:3-4 and in James 4:8.

_____

_____

_____

How can we see "hands" and "hearts" as an expression of our whole person?

_____

_____

_____

LAUGHTER TO MOURNING, HUMILITY TO HONOR

James 4:9-10 says, "Grieve, mourn and wail. Change your laughter to mourning and your joy to gloom. Humble yourselves before the Lord, and he will lift you up."

Read Amos 8:5-10 and Luke 6:24-25. What do these have in common with verses 9-10 from James 4?

_____

_____

_____

_____

In the passages from both Amos and Luke, what wrongdoing should people be mourning?

_____

_____

_____

_____

Where have we seen this theme earlier in James?

_____

_____

_____

_____

Read what Jesus says in Matthew 5:4 and 23:11-12. In light of James 4:9-10, why will those who mourn be comforted and those who are humbled be exalted?

_____

_____

_____

_____

What remedies for the fights and quarrels among us (mentioned in James 4:1) do we find in James 4:7-10?

_____

_____

_____

_____

Which of these would make the most difference for you and why?

_____

_____

_____

_____

---

[1]Scot McKnight, *The Letter of James,* New International Commentary on the New Testament (Grand Rapids: Eerdmans, 2011), p. 322.

[2]Job is not admitting guilt in 9:28-30. He's complaining that others have assumed his guilt so strongly that even if he washed, they still wouldn't consider him innocent. The point here is to note that Job gives an example of one way those in his day dealt with guilt—by washing and cleansing.

PART 3. REFLECT
Peacemakers Who Sow in Peace

Time magazine called it "possibly the widest ranging meeting of Christians ever held." In July 1974, in Lausanne, Switzerland, almost 4,000 Christians from 150 countries gathered, with half the delegates coming from the developing world. Under the sponsorship of Billy Graham, The International Congress on World Evangelization (what became known as Lausanne 74) convened to consider the implications of the Great Commission to make disciples of all nations for the twentieth century.

The planning committee asked John Stott to give the opening address and to draft a statement to present to the Congress that would summarize all the main talks presented. Stott was already the acknowledged leader of the evangelical wing of the Church of England and a respected international figure known for his leadership qualities and theological astuteness. But, with the very intentional diversity of the large gathering, this was a task to test even the most skilled diplomat.

For example, one of the issues in the air was that of evangelism and social action. The delegates were not unified on whether one of the pair had supremacy over the other, or whether one included the other, or whether one detracted from the other. In his opening address Stott said,

> Here then are two instructions, "love your neighbour" and "go and make disciples." What is the relation between the two? Some of us behave as if we thought them identical, so that if we have shared the Gospel with somebody, we consider we have completed our responsibility to love him. But no. The Great Commission neither explains, nor exhausts, nor supersedes the Great Commandment. . . . If we truly love our neighbour we

> shall without doubt tell him the Good News of Jesus. But equally if we truly love our neighbor we shall not stop there. . . . Love does not need to justify itself. It just expresses itself in service wherever it sees need.[1]

This was a very controversial statement for those who saw it as a threat to the call to evangelize. For those from developing countries, however, it was self-evident.

A small committee led by Stott sought to develop a statement for the Congress covering God, Christ, the Bible, the church, evangelism, social responsibility and more. Every day and often through the night they worked, submitting each paragraph to Billy Graham. The third complete draft was presented to the entire Congress for response. Three thousand replies were submitted, often of very diverging opinions.

After the committee seriously considered every reply, they revised, reworked and negotiated phrases and individual words, again often working through the night. Stott, as chair of the committee, presented the final document to the entire Congress. It incorporated a myriad of concerns in a unified fashion. While emphasizing the role of evangelism (with six of fifteen clauses focusing on that) it also affirmed, "The results of evangelism include obedience to Christ, incorporation into his Church and responsible service in the world. . . . The salvation we claim should be transforming us in the totality of our personal and social responsibilities. Faith without works is dead."[2]

Despite the disagreements along the way, 80 percent of the delegates signed their names to the statement. Stott's goal had been unity, but not at the cost of conviction. With utmost graciousness and perseverance, he was able to embrace both.

Stott's role as a peacemaker was not finished, however. Six months later a Lausanne Continuation Committee gathered in Mexico City. A movement arose among those present to make Graham the "Supreme President" of the Lausanne organization. Stott feared Third World delegates might be too deferential to Graham to voice their concerns regarding this move, even without Graham present. Indeed, how could Stott himself risk even the appearance of disrespect to perhaps the greatest evangelist of the twentieth century and someone for whom he had utmost admiration? Yet once again Stott spoke.

After affirming his personal affection for Graham, with whom he had had a twenty-year friendship, Stott suggested instead that there be several equal copresidents. Even the title "Supreme President," he said, could perpetuate images of Western paternalism that Lausanne had worked so hard to eliminate.

The next morning Stott met with Graham to explain personally what he had said during Graham's absence and why. After a full discussion, they went together to the meeting.

When they arrived, the atmosphere was tense. Some in the room thought Stott had made a power play. Others simply grieved the apparent split between two such revered leaders. Graham then stood before those assembled and read Psalm 133 and James 3:17-18: "The wisdom that comes from heaven is first of all pure; then peace-loving, considerate, submissive, full of mercy and good fruit, impartial and sincere. Peacemakers who sow in peace reap a harvest of righteousness." Having concluded that Stott was completely correct in this matter, Graham told the gathering that he declined the role sought for him and would accept nothing more than the title "Honorary Chairman."

We become the peacemakers James encourages us to be when, like Stott, we listen well and are "slow to speak." If we are slow to speak, then we have time and energy to focus on truly listening to what others are saying, to what the

Word of God is saying and to what the Spirit is saying. John Stott and Billy Graham were both models of listening. Stott showed that he was deeply concerned to hear what his Christian brothers from all over the world were saying—both in Lausanne and in Mexico City. Graham showed himself ready to listen to what his brother in Christ was saying. Indeed, when Stott died in 2011, Graham wrote, "Few people have influenced my life and ministry more than my good friend, John Stott."[3]

Listening, being slow to speak, is the first step in being peaceable and in being a peacemaker. Listening to others is an act of love. It is putting others ahead of ourselves—setting aside our agenda, goals and desires for as long as it takes to truly hear what the other person—or God himself—is saying. When we humble ourselves in this way, there is less opportunity for fights and quarrels to arise. Wrong motives and pride take a back seat.

Why is it often so difficult to show this kind of open love toward God and others? Why is it so easy to have wrong motives in a religious context? Often it comes down to our identity. Our core sense of worth and value can become rooted in what we do (as a student, designer, nurse, executive, teacher, etc.) or in a key role we fill (parent, spouse, caretaker, life of the party, etc.). When this is the case, watching our children rebel or failing in a project at work can be devastating. Or, when it looks like someone might replace us in a role as minor as chair of the church subcommittee on knives and forks, we can lash out in anger, blaming others for our situation.

We can also find our identity in our religious convictions. Our sense of value can be deeply imbedded in our beliefs and spiritual way of life. Humans are inevitably religious beings. What we believe in regard to these matters goes right to the center of our being. Which means we can be greatly troubled if others challenge what we are committed to or don't agree with us. *If what I believe is so clear, why don't others see it that way? If I'm wrong, have I wasted the time, energy and money I've devoted to this?* Feeling threatened, we tend to stay away from those who think differently than we do and associate with like-minded people. It's just safer that way.

But there can come times when interaction with those we disagree with is unavoidable, and the results can be, as James says, conflicts and disputes. We may try to get people removed from their positions of influence, damage their reputations in any way we can or insult them personally. We want them put down and put out of commission because of the threat they pose to us.

How, then, were John Stott and Billy Graham able to respond to disagreements and differences of opinions without being threatened, without anger or a desire to harm others, even while holding strong convictions themselves? The answer is that their identities were not in the positions or roles they possessed, or even in the beliefs they held. Their identity was in Christ. That is foundational to being a peacemaker. Stott and Graham knew deeply in their souls that they were loved by God and that his grace filled their lives. Nothing could take that away—not threats or disagreements or changes. Others might have believed differently. Others could have accused them of all kinds of things. They could have lost a job or a title. Ultimately, none of that mattered because God had said that through Christ they were his children, and nothing could ever separate them from Christ or his grace.

In Christ, peacemakers have the strength to be humble because they know the Lord has already lifted them up.

What's the main idea in this section?

What is one thing you can act on based on this reading?

[1]Timothy Dudley-Smith, *John Stott: A Global Ministry* (Downers Grove, IL: InterVarsity Press, 2001), pp. 211-12.
[2]The Lausanne Covenant, http://www.lausanne.org/en/documents/lausanne-covenant.html.
[3]Billy Graham in "Tributes," in *A Service of Thanksgiving for the Life of John R. W. Stott*, memorial service program, St. Paul's Cathedral, London, January 13, 2012, p. 18.

PART 4. DISCUSS
Putting It All Together

OPEN

Why do you think that fights and arguments erupt in even the best of families?

READ JAMES 3:13–4:10.

Often it is the people who love each other the most that fight the most. Husbands and wives, parents and children, brothers and sisters—it's all too common.

1. James addresses those who are wise and understanding among the readers. Compare what you've learned in part two about the expected conduct of those who are wise and understanding in Deuteronomy 1:13-18 to what James has said throughout the letter so far, and particularly what he says in 3:13.

2. What characteristics of earthly wisdom does James give in 3:14-16?

3. When have you seen earthly wisdom being the source of fights and quarrels?

4. When have you confused your own ambitions with your ambitions for God's work and purpose?

5. James said that the characteristics of heavenly wisdom would show themselves in good deeds and humility. Which of the seven characteristics of heavenly wisdom struck you as especially important and why?

6. In "Connect: Scripture to Scripture" we read that Isaiah speaks of the wisdom and understanding that will rest on the Messiah who will come and rule. We also considered Matthew 11:28-30, which describes the kind of leadership that Jesus exemplifies. Think about areas of responsibility you have—at church, in your family, at work, in school, with friends, in your community. How can you show evidence of your wisdom by fulfilling those tasks the way Jesus does and the way James recommends?

7. In what specific situations have you seen heavenly wisdom help resolve conflict?

8. What do you think it means that "peacemakers who sow in peace reap a harvest of righteousness"?

9. According to James in 4:1, fights and quarrels come from your desires that "battle" inside you. Reflect on a time when you were angry. What was going on inside you?

10. Why would James state that friendship with the world causes his readers to be adulterers in their relationship with God?

11. What do we need to be and do to come to God in prayer (4:7-10)?

12. How would each of these contribute to a humble spirit in you?

13. Consider the relationships in your life where there is regular tension, quarrels or hostility. What have you learned from this passage that will help you to engage in them in a different way?

Pray together about how you have gotten caught up in fighting recently. Talk to God about conflict in your life. Ask God to clear your mind of anger and distrust so that you can focus on his healing word.

GETTING PERSPECTIVE

James 4:11-17

WHERE WE'RE GOING

We have seen the theme of the importance of our words through-out James. Now he also takes a look at the topics of our attitudes toward others, God and the future through the lens of what we say. Our words can damage others outwardly and reveal the empty state of our inner selves. What we need is a healthy dose of perspective. Who really decides who is right or wrong? Who really has a say in what tomorrow will bring? Here's a clue: it's not you.

> Part 1. Investigate: James 4:11-17 (On Your Own)
>
> Part 2. Connect: Scripture to Scripture (On Your Own)
>
> Part 3. Reflect: Relying on God, Relying on Money (On Your Own)
>
> Part 4. Discuss: Putting It All Together (With a Group)

A PRAYER TO PRAY

Our God, you are the one who has given the Law. And you are the one who decides who has and who has not followed your ways. You are the one who guides our paths. It is not for us to make these decisions independent of you. Give us the grace to lay aside our pride, our false sense that we can live life without you. Give us humility that is seen in our words and in our deeds, that you may be glorified and that your people may be built up in love. Amen.

PART 1. INVESTIGATE
James 4:11-17

Read James 4:11-17.

1. What reasons does James give for not slandering or speaking against a Christian brother or sister (vv. 11-12)?

2. How do we tend to build ourselves up by criticizing others?

3. If we judge the law, what does this say about our attitude toward the lawgiver?

4. How can a proper attitude toward God (v. 12) enable us to have a proper attitude toward others?

5. How would you describe the two attitudes toward the future found in verses 13-17?

4:13-14 *Most of the wealth in the Roman Empire was accumulated by one of two means: the landed gentry, of high social class, made their wealth from land-based revenues such as tenant farmers and crops; the merchant class gathered great wealth without the corresponding social status. James addresses both merchants (4:13-17) and the landed aristocracy (5:1-6).*

6. James compares life to a mist (v. 14). How does a sudden death, especially that of a famous person, help us to realize this?

7. How do you respond emotionally to the idea that your life is like a mist?

8. How does knowing that your life is like a mist affect the way that you think about your future?

9. Is James saying it is wrong to plan for the future? Explain.

4:15-17. *"If God wills" was a conventional Greek expression but fit Jewish piety well; it appears elsewhere in the New Testament (e.g., Acts 18:21; 1 Corinthians 16:7).*

10. If you knew you were going to die tomorrow, how would your attitude and plans toward life today be different?

11. In verse 17 James says it is a sin not to do good when we know we should. In what areas of your life do you need to turn your plans over to God's will?

12. How can you cultivate humility in your attitude toward others and toward the future?

Ask God to help you love those around you rather than judge them. Humbly commit your future plans to the Lord.

PART 2. CONNECT
Scripture to Scripture

DO NOT SLANDER

We've already heard quite a bit about words and their destructive potential in the letter of James (1:19-21, 26; 3:1-12). But he isn't done yet. He has another angle to address on the topic.

Read Psalm 15 and list the godly behaviors that are mentioned in addition to not slandering, which we filled in for you.

1. _____   7. _____

2. _____   8. _____

3. _____   9. _____

4. Utters no slander   10. _____

5. _____   11. _____

6. _____   12. _____

Now read Psalm 50:16-20. List the behaviors associated with the wicked alongside slander.

1. _____   5. _____

2. _____   6. _____

3. _____   7. _____

4. _____   8. Slander your own mother's son

Given these positive and negative portraits, put into your own words a character profile of the kind of person the Bible has in mind when it mentions someone who slanders.

_____

_____

_____

_____

While *slander* could mean spreading gossip in Old Testament times, the word had a specific legal meaning in the justice system of ancient Israel, just like in the courts today. Leviticus 19:15-16 illustrates this, specifically mentioning slander in the context of court proceedings: "Do not pervert justice; do not show partiality to the poor or favoritism to the great, but judge your neighbor fairly. Do not go about spreading slander among your people." And one of the Ten Commandments on this kind of conduct is well known: "You shall not give false testimony against your neighbor" (Exodus 20:16).

Read Deuteronomy 19:15-21. In this court setting, what specific type of slander is mentioned?

_____

_____

How does this passage emphasize the seriousness of engaging in this type of slander?

_____

_____

_____

_____

Where else in James was taking others to court mentioned?

_____

_____

Summarize what was said there.

_____

_____

The Old Testament is not only concerned with outward behavior when it comes to slander but also with a person's inner state. How is the heart of someone who slanders others described in these two passages?

Psalm 101:3-5: _____

_____

Psalm 119:21-23: _____

_____

Now look at James 4:13-17. How is the inner condition of a person who slanders similar to someone who makes business plans without reference to God?

_____

_____

Why do you think this one inward state gives birth to both of these two different types of activities?

_____

_____

Consider times you've been critical toward others. Why does such a judgmental attitude have its roots in pride and arrogance?

_____

_____

As you consider your own critical attitude toward certain other people, take a moment to confess it to God and ask his forgiveness.

ONE LAWGIVER AND JUDGE

When James says "There is only one Lawgiver and Judge" in 4:12, he is once again (as he did in 2:19) hearkening back to the Shema, which we've looked at before—"Hear, O Israel: The LORD our God, the LORD is one. Love the LORD your God with all your heart and with all your soul and with all your strength" (Deuteronomy 6:4-5). As we mentioned previously, Jews recited this daily, emphasizing that there is one and only one God.

How do the very next verses in Deuteronomy 6 go on to highlight the importance of the Law that the one God gave them (see vv. 6-9)?

_____

_____

_____

_____

As we've already discussed, James referenced the two greatest commandments (see Mark 12:28-33) earlier in his letter; loving God is mentioned in James 1:12 and 2:5, and loving our neighbors is touched on in 2:8 and 18. We've just seen that he again alludes to the command to love God in 4:12. Where in James 4 does he once more reference Leviticus 19:18?

_____

_____

How do these two greatest commandments summarize all we really need to know about judging the way God desires?

_____

_____

_____

_____

_____

DO NOT JUDGE

The Old and New Testaments have an enormous amount to say about God as Lawgiver and Judge. Isaiah 33:22 explicitly ties these together: "For the LORD is our judge, the LORD is our lawgiver, the LORD is our king; it is he who will save us." God's people are to follow God not only in obeying the Law but also in the way they judge. While we don't have space here to go into detail on this huge topic that pervades the whole Bible, filling in this table will help us touch on a few things that especially relate to what James has to say.

	Characteristics of Judging That God Approves of or Disapproves of	Where This Theme Previously Appeared in James (give chapter and verse references)
Deuteronomy 1:16-17		
Proverbs 31:9		
Jeremiah 5:28		
Micah 3:11 and 7:3		

James writes, "Do not slander one another. Anyone who speaks against a brother or sister or judges them speaks against the law and judges it. When you judge the law, you are not keeping it, but sitting in judgment on it. There is only one Lawgiver and Judge, the one who is able to save and destroy. But you—who are you to judge your neighbor?" (4:11-12). How is slandering another the same as speaking against the law and judging it? Because to do so is to usurp God's role as Judge. In effect it is saying that the Law is wrong to claim that God is the Judge.

James's comments about judging are very reminiscent of Jesus' words in the Sermon on the Mount. What similarities and differences do you see between James 4:11-12 and Matthew 7:1-5?

_____

_____

_____

_____

Obviously James and Jesus both think they and God's people should distinguish between good behavior and bad behavior—and point out clearly to others when they are engaging in the one and not the other. What, then, do James (in 4:11-12) and Jesus (in Matthew 7:1-5) have in mind when they instruct us not to judge?

_____

_____

_____

_____

_____

What does it take to make sure that you exercise good judgment without being judgmental?

_____

_____

_____

_____

LIKE A MIST

James offers a vivid image of mist in 4:14 when he talks about the insecurity of plans we make without reference to God. And he points out that it's not just our plans but our entire lives that lack solidity!

In Psalm 1 we find a similar image. How does the psalmist express what life is like with and without God at the center?

_____

_____

_____

_____

The Bible is full of rich and poignant images that express the impermanence of life. This table highlights some of these. We've partially filled it in; you can do the rest.

	Who/What Is Temporary	Compared to What
Job 21:17-18	The wicked	
Psalm 1:4		Like straw before the wind
Psalm 37:20		
Psalm 39:5	My days	
		As nothing before You
	Everyone	
Psalm 39:6		
Psalm 68:1-2		
Psalm 102:3		
Psalm 102:11		
		Wither like grass
Proverbs 21:6		

	Who/What Is Temporary	Compared to What
Isaiah 17:13		
Hosea 13:2-3		
		Early dew that disappears
James 1:10-11		

As you consider these passages, what is your emotional reaction?

_____

_____

_____

_____

As a result, how are you moved to pray?

_____

_____

_____

_____

What dimensions does Jesus add to all this in Matthew 6:25-34?

_____

_____

_____

_____

THY WILL BE DONE

In James 4:13-17 we find a practical reason and a spiritual reason for being cautious about making plans. What's the practical reason?

_____

_____

_____

_____

What's the spiritual reason?

_____

_____

_____

Now read Proverbs 19:21 and 27:1. Which expresses a similar practical reason and which a spiritual one?

_____

_____

_____

One of the most well-known parts of the Sermon on the Mount, indeed of all of Scripture, is the Lord's Prayer found in Matthew 6:9-13. There we pray that God's will would be done on earth as it is in heaven. When it comes to our business plans and making money, what is God's will?

_____

_____

_____

One of James's main concerns in 4:13-17 is pride and arrogance (see especially 4:16). Think through each phrase of the Lord's Prayer. Express how each part offers an antidote to pride. *Our Father in heaven, hallowed be your name.*

_____

_____

_____

Your kingdom come, your will be done, on earth as it is in heaven.

_____

_____

_____

Give us today our daily bread.

_____

_____

_____

And forgive us our debts, as we also have forgiven our debtors.

_____

_____

_____

And lead us not into temptation, but deliver us from the evil one.

_____

_____

_____

Now prayer this prayer slowly, phrase by phrase, inserting the thoughts you've written down and relating these especially to your life and plans.

PART 3. REFLECT
Relying on God, Relying on Money

The four of us sat around our dining room table. We had enjoyed a good meal together and now we were enjoying some good conversation. Jack and Larry had been in a Bible study group with us for a few years, so it was not surprising that our discussion took a spiritual turn. Neither considered themselves Christians, but they were interested in Jesus and intrigued by what they saw in the Bible.

At one point, Jack turned to Larry and said, "You know, Larry, I know why I'm not a Christian, but I'm not sure I know why you're not."

We found Jack's honesty refreshing and were curious how Larry would respond. Without much hesitation, Larry answered. "That's easy. I've been told for forty years that I need to take care of myself and rely on myself. No one else is going to do it for me. So I've worked hard at my job and done my best to be successful. I've tried to make enough money to make sure I and my family have a good home, that my kids can have a solid education and that when I retire, there's enough left over for that too. Because, again, I can't count on anyone to bail me out when I'm a senior citizen.

"And now Phyllis and Andy here are telling me I need to rely on God. And Jesus says I need to depend not on myself but on him instead. And a lot of that makes sense and is in its own way appealing. But habits are hard to break. I've depended on myself for four decades. And I've been pretty successful at it too. The business decisions I've made have been profitable. I know how to get things done. So it's just a bit hard for me to see why I need the change."

We were struck by Larry's insight. While Larry had made his own decisions during his life, he was absolutely right that he was also following a way of thinking that his parents,

his education, in fact his whole culture had ingrained in his psyche. They had all told him subtly and overtly that the only person who is going to solve your problems and help you get ahead is you.

So deciding to turn his life over to God was not just a simple decision. It would require drastic change in his entire way of thinking and living. And why do it when he had been successful on his own for so long?

This kind of confidence is not just Larry's issue. People who are successful in business, for example, get used to things going the right way. Investments work out. Decisions prove profitable. Opportunities grow into realities. Life seems rock solid. This arrogance can be true for scholars and athletes and parents—almost anyone—as well.

But as James points out in 4:14, "Why, you do not even know what will happen tomorrow. What is your life? You are a mist that appears for a little while and then vanishes." And we all know this to be true. The rock star who seems to have it all dies suddenly. The business tycoon finds his young son has a deadly disease, and he can do nothing about it. The sports hero of yesterday doesn't know how to make the transition to a less famous lifestyle. The financial guru's investments suddenly turn to nothing.

Jesus also talks about how temporary the wealth of this world is. In Matthew 6:19 and 24 he says, "Do not store up for yourselves treasures on earth, where moths and vermin destroy, and where thieves break in and steal." We can never be completely in control. It is arrogant to imagine otherwise. It's an illusion.

What the rock star, the business tycoon, the sports hero and all the rest of us need is a massive infusion of perspective. There's nothing wrong with setting goals and making plans.

These can be valuable and healthy. The problem is presumption.

The pattern is all too familiar. An entrepreneur builds a huge, successful organization from nothing. An athlete at the peak of his powers earns tens of millions of dollars every year. They begin to think the usual rules do not apply to them. Ethics need not bind them. Relationships become expendable. The law is for other people. First they fall into the arrogance of presumption, and then they fall.

As James says, we must make a conscious effort to push back against this common tendency. We must be deliberate and intentional. Two Warrens give us a clue how—Rick Warren and Warren Buffett.

Rick Warren built one of the largest churches in America (Saddleback Church in Lake Forest, California) and wrote one of the bestselling books of all time (*The Purpose Driven Life*). Warren has made deliberate decisions to keep his lifestyle (and so his perspective on life) in check. As he told MSNBC news: "I still live in the same house I've lived in 16 years. I drive a 10-year-old Ford truck, bought my watch at Wal-Mart. You know, to me if you've got a good pair of jeans and a comfortable T-shirt, you don't have a whole lot of needs."[1]

The other Warren, the widely respected financial guru Warren Buffett, one of the richest men in the world, shows a similar sense of perspective. He is famous for his frugal lifestyle, still living in the same house he bought in Omaha, Nebraska, in 1958 for $31,500.[2] He has also become one of the champions of charitable giving among the super rich.

Our outward lives shape our inward character and vice versa. Living humbly is one way to help us be humble. And such an outlook has not kept Rick Warren or Warren Buffett from success. James urges us here to form mental, spiritual and practical habits that will shape our character, just as he did in chapter 1.

Those of us who have not seen mega-success can still exercise disciplines in life that help us maintain a healthy perspective on who we are and who God is. We as a couple have decided that giving a tenth of our income is a minimum. We have so much and God has been so generous with us, we believe that as stewards (not owners) of these resources, we have an obligation to give to others. We made this decision early in our married life when we had very little and have increased the percentage as time has gone on. Making a commitment to give early on has made giving easier (though still not easy) for us as our financial footing became stronger.

Every financial gift we make reminds us that the money was never ours to begin with. It is God's. He has given us life and health and opportunity. The thanks goes to him. Every gift we give is a reminder that he is God, and that we are not. It puts life in perspective. Eternal investments like these can never be lost like they can when we invest in real estate or stocks or gold or anything else.

Larry thought his ability to succeed and make his own way in life was what was permanent. He thought he could depend on himself. The money he had came from his own hand, not God's. Depending on himself—that, he thought, was solid.

Even as Larry thought he was in charge of his life because of his financial successes, he also thought he could not fail in relationships, in parenting or in his marriage. It wasn't many years following our dinner conversation that Larry, thinking he only had to rely on his own decisions, chose to live with another woman. He left his wife and beautiful children behind. This new woman, not too surprisingly, was not faithful to Larry either. She had a number of other men in her life; Larry was just one. But when all of this dawned on Larry and he realized how foolish he had been, it was too late. His wife, Carol, would not take him back. Larry's years of faithless behavior had borne fruit he never imagined. He didn't realize his life, a life in which he depended on himself, was a mist.

What's the main idea in this section?

What is one thing you can act on based on this reading?

[1]Quoted in Stoyan Zaimov, "Megachurch Pastors Use Their Millions to Bless Others," *The Christian Post,* February 1, 2012, accessed at http://www.christianpost.com/news/how-much-do-megachurch-pastors-make-68320/.
[2]Lisa Smith, "Warren Buffet's Frugal, So Why Aren't You?" Investopedia, January 5, 2010, accessed at http://www.investo pedia.com/articles/financialcareers/10/buffett-frugal.asp#axzz23wPhQGKM.

PART 4. DISCUSS
Putting It All Together

OPEN

Finish the sentence: When I think about my future I _____. (You might first all finish this sentence in a funny way, and then do a second round with a more serious answer.)

READ JAMES 4:11-17.

"I am the master of my fate. I am the captain of my soul." How subtly we convince ourselves that we control our lives. Sometimes only a crisis or even death itself convinces us otherwise. If we are truly wise and humble, we will listen carefully when James says, "You are a mist that appears for a little while and then vanishes."

1. In verse 11 James tells his readers, "do not slander one another." According to the following Old Testament passages, how seriously does God take slander?

   Deuteronomy 19:15-21

   Exodus 20:16

   Psalm 50:16-22

2. Why does James say we should not slander?

3. What motivates us to criticize each other?

4. The Law says that judgment belongs to God alone. To judge a brother or sister is to usurp God's role. Explain how a proper attitude toward God enables us to have the proper attitude toward others.

5. As we saw in "Connect: Scripture to Scripture," the Old Testament is not only concerned about the outward behavior of those who slander but the inward condition of the heart. How is the heart of one who slanders described in Psalm 101:3-5 and 119:21-23?

6. How is it that someone who slanders has a similar inner condition to someone who makes business plans without reference to God?

7. How do the two greatest commandments, to love God and each other, summarize all we need to know about judging the way God desires?

8. Obviously James and Jesus both think they and God's people should distinguish between good behavior and bad behavior—and point out clearly to others when they are engaging in the one and not the other. What, then, do James (in 4:11-12) and Jesus (in Matthew 7:1-5) have in mind when they instruct us not to judge?

9. Paraphrase the two attitudes toward the future that James describes in verses 13-17.

10. How is the attitude toward God described in verses 11-12 similar to that described in 13-17?

11. Do you agree that being generous shows a healthy attitude toward money and life? Why or why not?

12. How might James's declaration that your life is a mist that appears for a while and then vanishes affect the way you approach the coming week?

Think about what you have planned for the next month. Pray about each activity and commit it to God. Put each event under his care and ask him to guide you as he desires. Ask God if there are items he wants you to add or take off your schedule.

SESSION EIGHT

What Awaits

James 5:1-11

WHERE WE'RE GOING

Having taken on merchants in 4:13-17 James turns his attention in 5:1-6 to landowners. In reading this passage we can understand why someone has called James's letter "the Ouch! book."[1] James's words to the rich, to teachers and to the proud lay open every failing—not only for all of us to see, but also so that we can't help but see our own faults.

For those of us who suffer and await mercy, however, James has nothing but comfort and encouragement to offer. Wait for God, he counsels. Be patient, persevere. God is full of love and compassion. He will set all things right.

Part 1. Investigate: James 5:1-11 (On Your Own)

Part 2. Connect: Scripture to Scripture (On Your Own)

Part 3. Reflect: Wealth and Happiness (On Your Own)

Part 4. Discuss: Putting It All Together (With a Group)

A PRAYER TO PRAY

O Judge of all the earth, who brings armies to the defense of the defenseless, who is full of compassion and mercy for those who fear him, hear also our prayer. Forgive us for our greed, for our lack of concern for those in need. Forgive us for the times when we have not taken you seriously enough to take the people made in your image with deep seriousness as well. Forgive us for the ways we have criticized, demeaned or complained about our brothers and sisters in Christ. We may think them wrong, but we are certainly wrong to think we should be their judge instead of you. Forgive us for the sake of your kingdom. Forgive us out of your great mercy and compassion, that all may praise you and see that the Judge of all the earth does do right. Amen.

---

[1]George M. Stulac, *James*, InterVarsity Press New Testament Commentary (Downers Grove, IL: InterVarsity Press, 1993), p. 187.

PART 1. INVESTIGATE
James 5:1-11

Read James 5:1-11.

1. Into what two sections is this passage divided, and who is addressed in each?

2. James declares that misery awaits rich people. What crimes have they committed (vv. 1-6)?

3. Is James condemning all rich people? Explain.

4. Do you think of yourself as rich? Why or why not?

5. Look at verses 7-11. How is piling up riches the opposite of patience that waits in faith for God to provide?

6. When are you tempted to hoard rather than to give and wait on God?

7. Why do you think James begins the second section in verse 7 with "be patient"?

5:2. *Clothing was one of the primary signs of wealth in antiquity; many peasants had only one garment.*

5:4-6. *Throughout most of the rural areas of the Roman Empire, including much of rural Galilee, rich landowners profited from the toil of the serfs (often alongside slaves) who worked their estates.*

In first-century Palestine, many day laborers depended on their daily wages to purchase food for themselves and their families; withholding money could mean that they would go hungry.

The income absentee landlords received from agriculture was such that the wages they paid workers could not even begin to reflect the profits they accumulated. Although the rich supported public building projects (in return for attached inscriptions honoring them), they were far less inclined to pay sufficient wages to their workers.

5:7-8. *Harvest here (cf. v. 4) becomes an image of the day of judgment, as elsewhere in Jewish literature (especially 4 Ezra; Mt 13). Palestine's autumn rains came in October and November, and winter rains* *(roughly three-quarters of the year's rainfall) in December and January. But residents of Syria-Palestine eagerly anticipated the late rains of March and April, which were necessary to ready their late spring and early summer crops. The main wheat harvest there ran from mid-April through the end of May; the barley harvest was in March. The main grain harvest came in June in Greece, July in Italy. Farmers' families were entirely dependent on good harvests; thus James speaks of the "precious" (or "valuable"—NIV) fruit of the earth.*

5:11. *The whole structure of the book of Job was probably meant to encourage Israel after the exile; although God's justice seemed far away and they were mocked by the nations, God would ultimately vindicate them and end their captivity. Hellenistic Jewish tradition further celebrated Job's endurance (e.g., the Testament of Job, and Aristeas the Exegete). (Various later rabbis evaluated him differently, some positively, some negatively. The Testament of Job includes Stoic language for the virtue of endurance and transfers some earlier depictions of Abraham to Job; this transferral may have been the source of one later rabbi's rare conclusion that Job was greater than Abraham.)*

8. James goes on to give three examples of patient people: a farmer, the prophets and Job. How is each an example of patience?

9. In what areas of your life are you impatient?

10. In what ways could you learn patience from the three examples James mentions?

11. The Lord's coming provides a backdrop for James's word to the rich and to those who suffer. What different reactions would you expect each group to have to the prospect of the Lord's return mentioned in verses 7-9?

12. How does Christ's return affect such practical matters as our use of wealth and such emotional matters as our response to suffering?

Thank God for the practical help James gives in becoming more patient. Ask God to help you apply his message to the areas in your life that need patience.

PART 2. CONNECT
Scripture to Scripture

YOU RICH PEOPLE

The rich and the poor have not been far out of sight throughout the letter of James. The first in-kling comes when wisdom is mentioned in James 1:5. We saw that the Old Testament notion of wisdom that undergirded James's thought meant not just being wise, but being wise enough to obey God's laws, including his laws on dealing with the poor. In addition, wisdom for Old Testament rulers meant doing justice, especially for the poor (Jeremiah 7:5-7 and 22:3). James then brings this kind of wisdom to the forefront of his letter.

Look at each of the following passages on the rich and poor, and paraphrase in your own words the main idea you find in each.

James 1:9-11:

_____

_____

James 1:27:

_____

_____

James 2:1-7:

_____

_____

James 4:2:

_____

_____

James 4:13-17:

_____

_____

Why do you think this is such a major theme for James?

_____

_____

James hits the topic again in 5:1-6, even taking on the role of an Old Testament prophet in verse 1, perhaps more explicitly than anywhere else in his letter. His words and attitude are reminiscent of some of the hottest rhetoric of ancient Israel, such as Amos 4:1-3, in which the prophet roars against Samaria and gives warning about what will happen to the rich in the coming invasion:

> Hear this word, you cows of Bashan on Mount Samaria,
> > you women who oppress the poor and crush the needy
> > and say to your husbands, "Bring us some drinks!"
> The Sovereign LORD has sworn by his holiness:
> > "The time will surely come
> when you will be taken away with hooks,
> > the last of you with fishhooks.
> You will each go straight out
> > through breaches in the wall,
> > and you will be cast out toward Harmon,"
> > > declares the LORD.

In ancient Israel (as in most of the ancient world as a whole) most people lived just above a subsistence level; those who had a modest social or financial margin to help overcome random setbacks were considered wealthy. Any slight variation in rain or in the health of crops, any illness of livestock, any sickness or injury to family members who worked the fields and cared for the animals, any difficulty resulting from being taken advantage of by the wealthy, could be devastating for the poor. The least change could plunge a family into starvation and ultimately death. Like the Old Testament prophets, James was not willing to let that happen when there were some among God's people who could prevent it.

WEEPING AND WAILING

In James 5:1 he says the rich should weep and wail. In the Old Testament these signs of grief are of course associated with mourning the death of a loved one. But there are other reasons for them as well. Look up each of the following passages. Why is there weeping or wailing in each case?

Isaiah 13:6-9 (a prophecy against Babylon):

_____

_____

_____

_____

Isaiah 15:1-3 (a prophecy against Moab):

_____

_____

_____

_____

Joel 1:1-7 (concerning devastation in Israel):

_____

_____

_____

_____

What do these all have in common with James's use of "weep and wail" in James 5:1-6?

_____

_____

_____

_____

ROTTED, MOTH-EATEN AND CORRODED

Read what Jesus says in Matthew 6:19-21. What similarities do you see between Jesus' words and James 5:2-3?

_____

_____

_____

_____

As you consider your own life or the lives of others, when have you seen evidence of the truth of Jesus' statement that "where your treasure is, there your heart will be also"?

_____

_____

_____

_____

What are various ways you can store up permanent treasures in heaven?

_____

_____

_____

_____

A CONSUMING FIRE

When looking at James 3:6, we considered the range of meanings *fire* has in the Bible. Here in James 5:3 fire is clearly a sign of judgment. A number of places in the Old Testament also use fire to signify God's judgment. Look up the passages below and draw a line connecting each passage to the cause of God's judgment by fire that is mentioned. We got you started with Numbers 11:1-3.

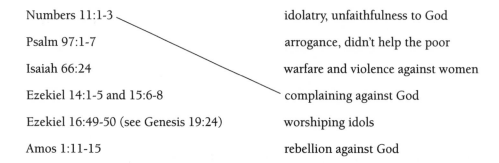

Numbers 11:1-3   idolatry, unfaithfulness to God

Psalm 97:1-7   arrogance, didn't help the poor

Isaiah 66:24   warfare and violence against women

Ezekiel 14:1-5 and 15:6-8   complaining against God

Ezekiel 16:49-50 (see Genesis 19:24)   worshiping idols

Amos 1:11-15   rebellion against God

Four of the passages noted above mention rejection of God—complaining against him, rebelling against him and worshiping idols. Two mention hostile actions toward others—not helping the poor, warfare and violence against women. In session four we saw how James has interwoven the two Great Commandments: to love God and love your neighbor. To disobey one is to disobey the other. In these Old Testament passages we see how disobedience of these two commands is interconnected, how one involves the other.

So look again at James 5:1-6. Why is selfish use of wealth a kind of idolatry deserving of judgment?

_____

_____

_____

_____

How can wealth, money or material possessions take priority over God and his ways in your life?

_____

_____

_____

_____

Read Matthew 13:38-43. What similar themes and ideas do you see here between the words of Jesus and the words of James in 5:1-6?

_____

_____

_____

_____

WAGES OF THE WORKER
Read Deuteronomy 24:14-15 and Leviticus 19:13. When were workers to be paid?

_____

_____

_____

_____

_____

As mentioned above, it was essential in ancient Israel that workers be paid daily because they had little or no savings or other financial safety net to see them through hard times. Worse than paying late is not paying laborers at all. Read Jeremiah 22:13-17. How does the prophet define what it means to know God?

_____

_____

_____

_____

_____

How does Malachi 3:5 make a similar point?

_____

_____

_____

_____

Why would fear of God lead us to pay fair wages, support those in need and ensure foreigners are dealt with compassionately?

_____

_____

_____

_____

James tells us in 5:4 what happens when the wages are not paid fairly: "The wages you failed to pay the workers who mowed your fields are crying out against you. The cries of the harvesters have reached the ears of the Lord Almighty." Crying out to God is frequently mentioned in the Old Testament. Consider just a few of those passages.

Old Testament Passage	Who did God hear cry out?	What was the cause of the cries?	What was God's response to the cries?
Genesis 4:8-12			
Exodus 2:23-24			
Psalm 34:17-20			
Psalm 72:11-14			

Consider the kinds of people who are crying out in these passages. Who are the people in like circumstances in your community?

_____

_____

_____

_____

What would their cries be?

_____

_____

_____

_____

How might your church or fellowship group be able to respond to one of these groups?

_____

_____

_____

_____

BE PATIENT

Given what immediately precedes James 5:7-9, what is James saying his readers should be patient about in verse 7?

_____

_____

_____

_____

This section at the end of James ties back to themes in the beginning of the letter. Look back at James 1:2-4 and 12. How are patience and perseverance similar?

_____

_____

_____

_____

Now read James 1:19 again. How is this verse related to the idea of patience?

_____

_____

_____

_____

Patience is a quality also associated with God. Read Nehemiah 9:29-31. How was God patient with his people?

_____

_____

_____

_____

See what the Old Testament says about how and why we are to be patient.

Old Testament Passage	What will be the result for those who have patience?	What themes do you see here that are also in James?
Psalm 37:5-9		
Proverbs 19:11		

When God is patient, he holds off judgment. He shows mercy to those who have stubbornly refused to obey him and honor him. Thus, when James talks about God's people being patient, he does not have in mind waiting in a long line without becoming annoyed and angry, and he isn't encouraging people to be at ease about an upcoming wedding or job change. He is saying that when we see evil and wickedness in the world, we must at the same time remember that judgment is in God's hands. Not ours. As the Lord says in Deuteronomy 32:35, "It is mine to avenge; I will repay. In due time their foot will slip." On the other hand, we can't simply ignore evil in the world. Are we to do nothing? No. We are to do what we can to stop wrongdoing and relieve its ill effects.

So we hold these two poles in tension. On the one hand we affirm that evil is truly evil by showing practical love to those who suffer because of it. At the same time we recognize that God is the only one who can judge and so we leave that to him. We work against evil while also refraining from self-righteous indignation and taking vengeance into our own hands. In this way we uphold the two Great Commandments.

In light of this understanding of patience, what events or circumstances do you need to be patient about?

_____

_____

_____

THE LORD'S COMING

In the first nine verses of chapter 5, James packs in no less than six references to judgment.

James 5:1	Weep and wail because of *the misery that is coming on you.*
James 5:3	You have hoarded wealth in *the last days.*
James 5:5	You have fattened yourselves in *the day of slaughter.*
James 5:7	Be patient, then, brothers and sisters, until *the Lord's coming.*
James 5:8	You too, be patient and stand firm, because *the Lord's coming* is near.
James 5:9	Don't grumble against one another, brothers and sisters, or *you will be judged. The Judge is standing at the door!*

"The day of the LORD" and similar phrases like "the day of destruction," the "day of rebuke" and the "day of vengeance" and even just "that day" are very common in the Old Testament. Here are just a few. Look up each passage below and fill in the missing words.

Isaiah 9:4:
 For as in the day of _____,
  you have shattered
 the yoke that burdens them.

Isaiah 13:1, 6:
A prophecy against _____ that Isaiah son of Amoz saw:

 . . . Wail, for the day of _____ is near;
  it will come like destruction from the Almighty.

Ezekiel 30:9:

On that day messengers will go out from me in ships to frighten Cush out of her
   complacency. Anguish will take hold of them on the day of _____
   doom, for it is sure to come.

Jeremiah 51:2:

I will send foreigners to _____
   to winnow her and to devastate her land;
they will oppose her on every side
   in the day of _____.

Zephaniah 1:4, 7:

I will stretch out my hand against _____
   and against all who live in _____. . . .
Be silent before the Sovereign LORD,
   for the day of _____ is near.

We see in these Old Testament passages that there was not just one "day of the Lord" but many
such days in different historical situations and regarding different nations, even against Israel.
That's why Amos says, "Woe to you [in Israel] who long for the day of the LORD! Why do you long
for the day of the LORD? That day will be darkness, not light" (5:18). Asking for God's judgment
to come, Amos warns, could be a request for God to judge his own people.

Thus, the "day of the Lord" in the Old Testament does not always refer to the final judgment or
to complete destruction. It can mean also mean a limited period of judgment. Given his firm
awareness of the Old Testament, James could have both of these kinds of judgment in mind when
he mentions "the coming of the Lord." He may be thinking of Christ's return at the end of the age.
But he may also be referring to the Lord coming to judge in a specific circumstance before the final
judgment. He certainly wants to communicate forcefully that God's justice as seen in the Old Testament comes to bear on the abuses he sees the rich of his own day piling on the weak.

Often we speak in the same way today. We may refer to certain fallen nations or leaders in history as having been subject to the Lord's judgment. But by this we don't necessarily mean the ultimate end of the age. Final judgment will certainly include a reckoning for all the righteous and all
the wicked. However, that need not always be the meaning of "the day of the Lord" when it's
mentioned in the Bible.

AUTUMN AND SPRING RAINS

Older translations of James 5:7 may use the terms "early" or "former" on the one hand and "latter,"
"later" or "late" rains on the other. Many more recent translations use "autumn" and "spring." Why
is this so? The "early" or "former" rains refer to the autumn rains of September and October (see
Joel 2:23). The "latter" rains are in the spring months of March and April. While the Jewish calen-
dar begins in the month of Nisan (March-April), the agricultural year of planting begins in the fall
and continues till spring when a second season of rain occurs. After the heat of summer dries up
the landscape, the cycle starts again in the fall. So the autumn rains are first ("former") and the
spring rains are second ("latter") in the cycle.

In the ancient Near East, as today, rain is a precious element for life and health. In an agrarian

society, rain for crops and water for domestic animals as well as for people is critical. It is not surprising, then, that rain took on sacred significance. Fill in the table to get a sense of this.

Old Testament Passages	What condition is mentioned?	What will God then do in response?	What is the result of God's response?
Leviticus 26:3-5			
Deuteronomy 11:13-15			
Deuteronomy 28:1-2, 12			

Rain is associated with God's blessing, and God's blessing is linked to obedience to his commands. With this in mind we can see that when James encourages his readers to wait patiently as
farmers do for the rain, he is counseling them to both obey God and wait for his blessings.

James of course did not think that obedience meant there would be no hardship or trial. God is
not a celestial candy machine. We should not think that if we put in the right spiritual coinage that
God must necessarily dispense a divine sweet to us. Material and physical adversity may come. As
indicated by James 1:2, one of the main reasons he seems to be writing his letter is to explain why
such difficulties come to those who love and obey God. It's also clear from what we've just read in
5:1-6 that he knows God's righteous people were oppressed by the rich. And back in James 1 he
tells us we should not be surprised when trials come but should endure them faithfully. From such
perseverance, though, James assures us God's blessings do come: blessings like maturity, wisdom
and "the crown of life" (James 1:4-5, 12). God is indeed faithful.

What blessings have you seen come to you in the midst of difficulties or trials—or perhaps even
because of these?

_____

_____

_____

DON'T GRUMBLE

The theme of judgment continues in James 5:9. But instead of focusing on the rich, James now
turns the target of his attention to the Christian community. While others such as the rich may
deserve condemnation, we should not think we are excluded from God's evaluation.

How is grumbling against each other a link between the themes of patience (in 5:7-8) and perseverance (in 5:10-11)?

_____

_____

_____

James has already raised the theme of speaking against fellow Christians in 4:11-12. There too he connects this kind of destructive speech to the reality of God as our Judge. Just as the rich bring harm to the weak, so our words can bring harm to others.

Why is it so easy to fall into a habit of complaining about fellow Christians—those within our immediate fellowship and well-known Christian leaders or groups we may know of?

_____

_____

_____

_____

What needs to change within you in order for you to become someone who grumbles less about others?

_____

_____

_____

_____

How can you develop new patterns to replace your habits of complaining?

_____

_____

_____

_____

THE EXAMPLE OF THE PROPHETS

Do things always go well for God's people, for those who obey God? As we mentioned above, James says no. In fact, in verse 5:10 he points out that the prophets themselves suffered *for* obeying God. To get a picture of this, fill in the missing spaces in the table, which highlights some suffering prophets.

Old Testament Passages	The Prophet(s)	How the Prophet(s) Suffered
Jeremiah 20:1-2	Jeremiah	
Jeremiah 26:20-23		
1 Kings 18:4	The LORD's prophets	
2 Chronicles 24:20-21		Stoned to death

How is what James writes in 5:10-11 similar to Jesus' teaching in Matthew 5:11-12?

_____

_____

_____

_____

What similar themes are also found in Matthew 23:37?

_____

_____

_____

_____

In Matthew 23:37 Jesus compares himself to these same prophets who, out of great love for the people of Israel, brought the sometimes unpopular message of God's word. He also compares himself to a mother hen who wants to gather her chicks around her to protect them from harm, whether it be from a fox or a barnyard fire. Thus, we can take encouragement not just from the example of the prophets but also from that of our Lord Jesus Christ. He suffered not for the sake of suffering nor merely to prove a point; he suffered because of his great love for God and for us.

THE PERSEVERANCE OF JOB

Since the book of Job is one of the longer books of the Old Testament, we won't be able to look at it all. To summarize briefly, in the first two chapters we see Satan challenging God in the heavenly courts. God's servant Job is faithful to him, claims Satan, only because of all the blessings he has. Take those away, says the Accuser, and Job will curse God. So God allows Satan to destroy Job's large family, his substantial wealth and ultimately his health.

In chapters 3–37 Job and four friends (not knowing of the heavenly challenge) then discuss back and forth the nature of God and reasons for suffering. At the nub is whether these calamities were due to Job's sin (as his friends accuse) and how God is just, along with Job's cry for his own audience with God to plead his case. Finally, in 38:1–42:6 God replies to Job, proclaiming his mighty power over the universe and setting himself in contrast to Job, who is just one of his humble creations. That God does not directly respond to the issues raised in the middle chapters suggests that those are not the right questions to ask. While God is sovereign, the created order is a mix of good and evil which does not reflect his justice at every point. Bringing God's truth and shalom to the earth is a long process, and we will not see complete restoration until the very end. The last verses of Job 42 tell of Job's restored fortunes.

Read Job 1:20-22 and 2:9-10, which follow the accounts of Job's losses. How does Job show his perseverance here?

_____

_____

_____

_____

James says his readers know what the Lord finally brought about for Job. Read the epilogue to the book in Job 42:10-17. What are the key elements of Job's final outcome?

_____

_____

_____

_____

As mentioned above, here at the end of his letter, James returns to his opening theme of finding joy in perseverance in Christ. He had urged his readers to count it all joy when they met various trials because the testing of faith produces perseverance (1:2-3). Now, near his conclusion, he says, "We count as blessed those who have persevered" (5:11). What blessings do you see in continuing faithfulness to Christ even when there are difficulties?

_____

_____

_____

_____

PART 3. REFLECT
Wealth and Happiness

"¡Mucho gusto! ¡Mucho gusto!" We were surrounded by smiles and welcomed with handshakes, hugs and kisses from dozens of total strangers. Adults greeted us warmly and children literally hung on us. Everywhere we went it was the same. Young and old were happy to see us as we used what little Spanish we knew and they used what little English they had.

We were visiting our daughter Susan, who was in Peru for two years working with a church among the poor in the large coastal city of Chimbote. She had become fluent in Spanish and lived with a family in San Luis. Even though we might call it a barrio, the Peruvians, always hopeful about the future, called it a *pueblo joven* or "young town." Susan's work included connecting the residents to what little medical care was available and assisting with Christian education for the children.

At the time we visited San Luis, about twenty-five thousand people lived there in mostly one-story cinderblock homes. The streets were wide but unpaved—just dust. Technically the people were squatters, but the government tolerated their presence and would eventually grant them ownership of land no one else made use of.

We were welcomed into the homes of several families. Each house had dirt floors and a few pieces of furniture. Often they had electricity ("borrowed" from the grid) for lights, a television and maybe a refrigerator. What little they had they proudly shared with us, especially Inca Kola, the national soft drink of Peru.

They possessed a cheerful attitude even though they were usually underemployed or unemployed. Often they made do selling trinkets or bottles of water or other basic goods in the street. Life was not easy and there was much heartache. The Peruvians had assorted problems, some of which they brought on themselves. But love seemed to spring from them unbidden. Children seemed to be everywhere—full of laughter, playing games, singing songs, hugging each other and us.

Just once during our visit did we encounter an unhappy, crying child. It was not in the orphanage nor in the school that Susan also worked in. Instead it was toward the end of our trip when we were visiting the American-style mall in Miraflores in Lima with nicely dressed Peruvians strolling amid the upscale shops along the Pacific coast. There a well-to-do Peruvian couple was walking with two young boys. One of them was upset with his parents for not letting him do what he wanted; he wanted something and they said no, so he yelled and cried and pulled against his parents who unsuccessfully tried to settle him down.

We've never witnessed a more vivid parable that money cannot buy happiness. Now, it would be perverse to conclude that the residents of San Luis and thousands of similar communities around the world should be left in their deprived state so they can be happier. To paraphrase Paul in Romans 6:1-2, "Shall we allow people to continue in poverty so they can have more joy? By no means!"

Our call as Christians is clear: Where there is suffering, bring relief. Where there is unemployment, honorable work. Where there are laws that support the rich at the expense of the poor, justice. Where there is ignorance, education. Where there is sickness, medical care. And this has been the history of the church for the last two thousand years. Wherever Christians have gone around the world they have built hospitals and schools. Today they dig wells to provide clean water and support microenterprises so people in otherwise dire circumstances can earn a living wage.

Our wealth is not for ourselves alone. And

it is certainly not to push people down even further, as James condemned the rich of his day for doing. Even withholding one day's pay could be disastrous for people on the edge of ruin in the ancient world of the Bible.

That's the backdrop to the parable of the workers in the vineyard that Jesus told in Matthew 20:1-16. The landowner went out to hire workers in the morning. Later he saw more in the marketplace doing nothing and hired them. As the day went on he did this a third, fourth and fifth time—hiring the last group at five in the afternoon. At the end of the day he paid them all the same.

Now we know this as a story of God's abundant grace. But Jesus' first listeners would have known that for people who were chronically unemployed, getting paid at the end of the day was both expected practice and essential. In a society without enough jobs to go around, these workers were living day to day. They had no savings, no relatives to fall back on. Without that pay, their families would literally go hungry. It was a matter of life and death. Thus James condemns the rich for withholding pay even one day.

In Peru we saw this exact same scenario played out. There were customary street corners in the center of town where men hung out, waiting and hoping for someone to come along to hire them for the day. And those needing laborers would swing by in their pickup trucks, load up as many as were needed, and drive off to a farm field, a construction site or the loading docks at the wharf. At the end of the day, these workers were paid. The next day, the cycle was repeated.

Treating workers fairly, showing mercy to the oppressed, offering the gospel of peace and hope—all of these things are equally spiritual activities. James indicates his concern with these matters when he calls for employers to pay their workers each day as is so essential for them.

Often we think of our relationship with God as what is truly spiritual. We are not re-futing that; we know there is nothing more important or glorious than knowing God. As J. I. Packer so famously and movingly puts it in his classic book *Knowing God*:

> What were we made for? To know God.
>
> What aim should we set ourselves in life? To know God
>
> What is the "eternal life" that Jesus gives? Knowledge of God. "This is eternal life: that they may know you, the only true god, and Jesus Christ, whom you have sent" (Jn 17:3).
>
> What is the best thing in life bringing more joy, delight and contentment than anything else? Knowledge of God. "This is what the LORD says: 'Let not the wise man boast of his wisdom or the strong man boast of his strength or the rich man boast of his riches, but let him who boasts boast about this: that he understands and knows me'" (Jer 9:23-24).[1]

But what does it mean to *know* God? To simply have mere information about God? Packer makes it clear that that's not even near the mark. Much closer is to have a loving, trusting relationship with him. But perhaps somewhat surprisingly Jeremiah 22:15-16 does not equate knowing God with either of these. Here is what Jeremiah said to the king of Judah:

> "Does it make you a king
>   to have more and more cedar?
> Did not your father have food and
>   drink?
>   He did what was right and just,
>   so all went well with him.
> He defended the cause of the poor and
>   needy,
>   and so all went well.
> Is that not what it means to know me?"
>   declares the LORD.

In Malachi 3:5 we find the same sentiment, just stated in the negative:

> "So I will come to put you on trial. I will

be quick to testify against sorcerers, adulterers and perjurers, against those who defraud laborers of their wages, who oppress the widows and the fatherless, and deprive the foreigners among you of justice, but do not fear me," says the LORD Almighty.

Who are the people who don't fear God, who don't know him well enough or who don't have a deep enough relationship with him to care whether they obey him or not? The people "who defraud laborers of their wages, who oppress the widows and the fatherless, and deprive the foreigners among you of justice." Weeping and wailing is what awaits such people when God takes them to court.

So we might also add to J. I. Packer's list of what it means to know God:

> What does knowing God look like? That we obey God by defending "the cause of the poor and needy."

We would be wrong to say knowing God has nothing to do with prayer, with reading Scripture, with joining others in worship, with the forgiveness of sins or with the salvation that comes to us freely through Christ. But, as Jeremiah and Malachi tell us, it would be equally wrong to say that helping marginalized people also has nothing to do with knowing God. These are two sides of the same coin, two wings of the same airplane.

Once again we see how the two Great Commandments are intimately connected, virtually one. We can't claim to love God if we don't show love toward those in need. At the same time, loving our neighbors without leaning on and relying on God leads to cynicism and burnout. It can make us judgmental and full of criticism for those who don't help us in such work—even fellow believers. It can leave us angry and, yes, impatient.

The apostle says in James 5:1 that sorrow and misery await the rich who are greedy and break the law for their own gain. Money can't buy ultimate happiness. But money can be used to pay people justly, to care for those in need, to express God's loving generosity. When we do, we can find contentment, peace and even joy, as our Peruvian friends did, in the midst of suffering.

What's the main idea in this section?

What is one thing you can act on based on this reading?

---

[1]J. I. Packer, *Knowing God* (Downers Grove, IL: InterVarsity Press, 1973), p. 33.

PART 4. DISCUSS
Putting It All Together

OPEN

How does the culture set your agenda and determine your lifestyle?

READ JAMES 5:1-11.

1. Review what James says about the poor and rich throughout his letter: 1:9-11, 27; 2:1-7; 4:2, 13-17 and now in 5:1-6. Why do you think the poor and rich is such a major theme for him?

2. In verses 1-6 James declares that misery awaits rich people to the point that they should weep and wail. What are they guilty of?

3. When has wealth or material possessions taken priority over God and his ways in your life?

4. The reading in part three considers the old saying, "Money can't buy happiness." If that's so, how can we gain happiness?

5. Given what immediately preceded verses 7-9, why would James ask his brothers and sisters to be patient until the Lord's coming?

6. Describe how each of the following are effective examples of patience:

    farmers

    the prophets

    Job

7. How is piling up riches the opposite of patience?

8. The Lord's coming provides a backdrop for James's words to the rich and to those who suffer. How do you think each group would have reacted to the prospect of the Lord's return mentioned in verses 7-9?

9. How does Christ's return affect such practical matters as our use of wealth and such emotional matters as our response to suffering?

10. Why is the admonition to not grumble against each other placed between two thoughts on patience?

11. What specifically would you like to learn from the prophets and Job as examples of those who lived patient lives?

12. How have you experienced the Lord's compassion and mercy in times of suffering?

Give thanks to God for his grace and strength in times of difficulty. Ask God to help you know how to use your money well and where you should be seeking happiness.

BECOMING WHOLE

James 5:12-20

WHERE WE'RE GOING

In these final verses of the letter of James, we find several topics: taking oaths, prayer and helping those who wander. Many commentators see little connection among them. Others think they do tie in with each other and with what has gone before.

Certainly James has shown proverb-like qualities in his writing—as well as strong thematic links to the book of Proverbs itself. He often moves quickly from one topic to another, offering succinct axioms, instructions and wise sayings, much like Proverbs. As we study these final verses, one thing we'll explore is whether the topics represent what James wanted to say but couldn't find any logical place for earlier or if he placed them here at the end intentionally.

Part 1. Investigate: James 5:12-20 (On Your Own)

Part 2. Connect: Scripture to Scripture (On Your Own)

Part 3. Reflect: Call the Elders of the Church to Pray (On Your Own)

Part 4. Discuss: Putting It All Together (With a Group)

A PRAYER TO PRAY

God of heaven and earth, we give you thanks that your love encompasses all of who we are—body, soul and spirit. You desire and have made a way for us to enjoy your peace, your shalom, in our lives. Whether we are faced with sickness or sin, broken relationships or trying circumstances, you are the one who upholds us, heals us, forgives us. Give us the love and strength to pray for each other, confess our sins to each other and bring each other back to your truth. Grant this so that your name may be glorified in our lives, in our church, in our world. We pray all this in your name. Amen.

PART 1. INVESTIGATE
James 5:12-20

Read James 5:12-20.

1. How do the instructions in verse 12 reinforce the themes of
   the tongue (3:1-12) and of patience (5:9-11)?

2. What different kinds of prayer are mentioned in this passage?

3. What experiences have you had with these kinds of prayer in
   your life?

4. What steps could you take to make at least one of these types
   of prayer more a part of your life?

5. In verses 14-16 James discusses physical and spiritual healing. What are the steps in this process?

6. How is physical healing connected with forgiveness of sins?

7. Would you call elders or other church leaders for anointing,
   prayer and confession? Why or why not?

5:14. *Wounds were anointed
with oil to cleanse them (cf.
Lk 10:34), and those with
headaches and those
wishing to avoid some
diseases were anointed with
olive oil for "medicinal"
purposes (from the ancient
perspective). Oil was also
used to anoint priests or
rulers, pouring oil over the
head as a consecration to
God. Christians may have
combined a symbolic
medicinal use with a symbol
of handing one over to the
power of God's Spirit (Mk
6:13).*

5:17-18. *Although all Palestinian Jews prayed for rain, few miracle workers were thought able to secure such answers to prayer. . . . The miracle of securing rain eventually came to be viewed as equivalent to raising the dead. The piety of these miraculous rainmakers always set them apart from others in Jewish tradition, but here James affirms that Elijah, the greatest model for such miracle workers, was a person like his readers and is a model for all believers (1 Kings 17:1; 18:41-46; cf. 1 Sam 12:17-18; for Elijah's weakness cf. 1 Kings 19:4).*

8. How can we provide other opportunities for mutual confession and prayer (v. 16)?

9. How does the Old Testament prophet Elijah illustrate the effectiveness of prayer (vv. 17-18)?

10. Elijah was a person just like us. In what ways do you struggle as you attempt to grow in prayer?

11. According to verses 19-20, how, if at all, are we responsible for one another?

5:19-20. *In Jewish belief, the former righteousness of one who turned away was no longer counted in his or her favor (Ezek 18:24-25), but (in most Jewish formulations) the repentance of the wicked canceled out his or her former wickedness (Ezek 18:21-23), if conjoined with proper atonement. Some Jews (Dead Sea Scrolls, some rabbis) regarded some forms of apostasy as unforgivable, but James welcomes the sinner back. In this context, he is especially inviting revolutionaries to return to the fold.*

12. Summarize what verses 13-20 teach us about how we can help people become whole physically, emotionally or spiritually.

13. How would you like to be more involved in this kind of ministry?

Ask God for grace as you minister to others.

PART 2. CONNECT
Scripture to Scripture

YES AND NO

While "above all" in James 5:12 is also translated "most important" (CEB) or "most of all" (NLT), this is a customary phrase that is used to mean "finally."[1] So James is merely alerting his readers that he is about to wrap things up. He begins his concluding remarks with the topic of making oaths.

When James mentions swearing "by heaven" (5:12) he's referring to a custom among the Jews that we mentioned in session three. Because Jews wanted to be sure they did not, even accidentally, break the commandment about taking the Lord's name in vain, they refrained from saying his name at all. Instead they used a number of substitutes for *Yahweh*, most commonly "the LORD." Another euphemism for *God* is "heaven," as when the prodigal son says he "sinned against heaven," by which he means he sinned against God.

Fill in the table for an overview of what the Old Testament says about using the Lord's name.

Old Testament Passage	What is said about using the Lord's name or taking an oath before the Lord?
Exodus 20:7	
Leviticus 19:12	
Exodus 22:10-11	
Deuteronomy 6:13	

How are the first two passages listed above different from the next two?

_____

_____

_____

_____

How would you summarize, then, the Old Testament teaching on using the Lord's name?

_____

_____

_____

_____

James's prohibition of swearing oaths is reminiscent of Jesus' teaching in the Sermon on the Mount. Read Matthew 5:33-37. What similarities do you see between this passage and James's teaching?

_____

_____

_____

_____

What added detail does Jesus give that is not found in James 5:12?

_____

_____

_____

_____

Read Matthew 23:16-22. When talking about swearing oaths, Jesus clearly has in view the many restrictions and requirements that the Pharisees had added to the Law. Here is an example of rules and regulations multiplied out of control. Jesus and James aim to cut through the morass in order to refocus attention on what truly is at stake, which was in danger of being lost. What is the core idea about our speech that Jesus wants to emphasize in Matthew 5:33-37 and that James also emphasizes in 5:12?

_____

_____

_____

_____

Craig Keener writes about James 5:12, "The idea is probably that one should not impatiently (5:7-11) swear; rather one should pray (5:13). One should pray rather than swear because the fullest form of an oath included a self-curse, which was like saying 'May God kill me if I fail to do this' or (in English preadolescent idiom) 'Cross my heart and hope to die.'"[2]

PRAYING IN TIMES OF TROUBLE
Throughout his letter, James has mentioned a variety of difficulties believers can find themselves in. Look up these passages and draw a line connecting each passage to the kind of trouble it describes.

James 1:2-4	being poorly clothed and hungry
James 1:12-14	not being paid fairly
James 1:26-27	temptations
James 2:14-17	various trials
James 5:1-6	being a widow or orphan

Look back at James 1:2-8 and at what James says we should do when we find ourselves in various trials. How is this similar to 5:13?

_____

_____

_____

_____

What troubles do you need to bring to the Lord now?

_____

_____

_____

_____

Pause a moment to pray.

SONGS OF PRAISE

When we are in trouble, prayer can come much more readily to us. We deeply feel our need of God and his aid in such times. Ironically, we might be less likely to pray when we experience God's blessing.

Many psalms exhort us to sing praise to God just as James does in 5:13. Just a few are found below. Note the reasons given for praising God in each psalm. We filled in the first one for you.

Psalms	Reasons for Praising God
Psalm 28:6-7	He heard my cry for mercy. He is my strength, my shield.
Psalm 65:5-8	
Psalm 95:1-5	
Psalm 96:1-3	
Psalm 100:1-5	
Psalm 149:1-5	

What other reasons would you add for praising God?

_____

_____

_____

_____

Take a moment to praise God for all these things.

ANOINTING WITH OIL

Oil had many practical purposes in the ancient world. It was used for cooking, for medicine and as fuel for lamps. It was also used in the Old Testament as a sign of many things, such as joy, God's blessing and the presence of God. Being anointed with oil was a sign of being consecrated (set apart) for the Lord or his work as well. This finds its greatest expression in the names *Messiah* (in Hebrew) and the equivalent word *Christ* (in Greek), which mean "Anointed One."

Read the passages and circle the word or phrase that describes what is symbolized by oil in each case. Sometimes a passage includes more than one.

Deuteronomy 11:13-15	Joy	God's Blessing	Presence of God	Consecrated to Lord's Work
Job 29:1-6	Joy	God's Blessing	Presence of God	Consecrated to Lord's Work
1 Samuel 16:12-13	Joy	God's Blessing	Presence of God	Consecrated to Lord's Work
Psalm 23:5-6	Joy	(God's Blessing)	(Presence of God)	Consecrated to Lord's Work
Psalm 45:1, 7-8	Joy	God's Blessing	Presence of God	Consecrated to Lord's Work
Isaiah 61:1-3	Joy	God's Blessing	Presence of God	Consecrated to Lord's Work
Joel 2:19-20	Joy	God's Blessing	Presence of God	Consecrated to Lord's Work

Summarize in your own words what oil means in these Old Testament passages.

_____

_____

_____

With regard to healing, oil had a direct medical benefit. It was used internally for digestive problems and externally to clean out and soften wounds, as well as to soothe injuries (as in the parable of the good Samaritan in Luke 10:34). So it was natural that oil would become a symbol of God's presence to heal spiritually and physically, to restore joy, and to renew us for the work he has called us to.

In this same manner, sin and sickness were often closely associated in the Old Testament.

In Psalm 38:1-3 and Psalm 41:1-4, for example, David seems to inextricably link a sick body with his sin. (See also, as another example, Leviticus 26:14-16.) It makes sense, then, that forgiveness is linked with healing. Psalm 103:2-3 reads, "Praise the LORD, my soul, and forget not all his benefits—who forgives all your sins and heals all your diseases."

It's therefore not surprising that in 5:15 James also links sin and sickness, forgiveness and heath. What are examples today of links between sinful behavior and health problems?

_____

_____

_____

Perhaps you thought of examples like abusing your body by smoking, which can lead to cancer or emphysema. If you didn't do so above, note how wrong choices about attitudes or relationships can also affect our health negatively.

_____

_____

_____

PRAYER, SICKNESS AND FORGIVENESS

James 5:15 raises a number of challenging issues. If the prayer of faith makes a person well, do people die and get sick because of our lack of faith? And what about the connection between physical sickness and spiritual sickness? Is there always a link between the two? Are all illnesses caused by sin?

While James does follow an Old Testament line of thought that links sin and sickness, this is not the only perspective found in the Old Testament or the New. First, consider the book of Job, which we looked at briefly in session eight. Job's friends say that his calamities, including his physical illness, are due to sin. Eliphaz advises Job, "Blessed is the one whom God corrects; so do not despise the discipline of the Almighty" (5:17). Zophar tells him God afflicts him less than his sin deserves (11:6). Job responds to these and other accusations with a claim of innocence: "How many wrongs and sins have I committed? Show me my offense and my sin" (13:23).

At the end of the book, God shows up and sets the record straight. Read Job 42:7-9. What does God say to Eliphaz?

_____

_____

_____

God suggests that sometimes there is an explanation other than sin for why bad things happen to good people. Jesus was confronted with this same question and with the mindset of Job's friends. Read John 9:1-7. What all does Jesus say about why the man was born blind?

_____

_____

If illness is not always caused by sin, can illness always be cured by the prayer of faith? The apostle Paul encountered this issue in his own life. Read 2 Corinthians 12:7-10. We can safely assume that the great apostle did not lack faith. Just prior to this (2 Corinthians 11:16–12:6), Paul tells about his feats of faith in enduring suffering and persecution, and also enjoying astonishing visions of paradise. The Lord responds to Paul's request for healing by saying no, however. What reason is given (12:9-10)?

_____

_____

How have you seen God's glory displayed through faith (your own or someone else's) in the midst of illness or struggles?

_____

_____

_____

_____

Above we reviewed the different kinds of troubles faced by Christians that James mentions: trials, temptations, being widowed or orphaned, being poorly clothed and hungry, not being paid fairly. In some of these cases, there is another cause besides our sin; we are not always the source of our own troubles. Sometimes it is the sin of others—the rich who oppress, the Satan who accuses, those opposed to Christ who persecute.

So when bad things happen, what do we do? James tells us clearly. If we are in trouble—pray. If we are sick—call the elders to pray. If we have sinned—confess.

And indeed, because of this encouragement to pray for physical healing, we should eagerly do so when the situation presents itself. God is good and desires to do good in our lives. But we need to do so with a sense of humility, recognizing that we are not God, that we do not know his purposes in all circumstances, and that we are never in a place to accuse others of a lack of faith. Even Paul's prayers for healing were not answered.

In the same vein, because James does say—and the Old Testament agrees—that there can be a significant link between sin and sickness, we should be alert to this possibility as we minister to others. But we should never be overconfident in our analysis, and never quick to assume illness is the result of sin, like Job's friends did. As Jesus taught his disciples, sometimes "neither this man nor his parents sinned." Instead, we humbly look to God in faith and trust him for the results.

CONFESS YOUR SINS

James 5:16 calls for us to confess our sins to one another. There are several great psalms of confession. We'll look briefly at just two.

Read Psalm 32. How does the psalmist describe the results of not confessing (vv. 3-4)?

_____

_____

_____

_____

What happens once the psalmist confesses (32:5)?

_____

_____

_____

_____

What does the psalmist conclude about confession and about God as a result of receiving forgiveness (32:6-11)?

_____

_____

_____

_____

Read Psalm 51. What does the psalmist ask of God in 51:1-12?

_____

_____

_____

_____

How does he say he will then respond (51:13-15)?

_____

_____

_____

_____

Both psalms tell us that being forgiven is not the end of the process. It is the beginning of a new stage of reaching out to others. Think of a time you received forgiveness. How did things change for you as a result?

_____

_____

_____

_____

Confessing sins to one another is not common in the Protestant tradition despite James's injunction to do so and Jesus' confirmation to the apostles in John 20:23 that "if you forgive anyone's sins, their sins are forgiven; if you do not forgive them, they are not forgiven." As James suggests, confession need not be to someone who is ordained. It can be to any mature Christian in a safe and confidential environment.

Richard Foster suggests three advantages to a formal time of confession. First, it doesn't allow us to make excuses and not take responsibility for ourselves. Second, we hear the word of absolution or forgiveness from Scripture from a living being. This reinforces vividly the assurance of

God's love and our reconciliation with him. Third, it helps us come to terms with the sinfulness of sin so that we might move closer to the holiness of God.[3]

Describe a time when you confessed your sin to a fellow Christian. What was the experience like? If you've never done that before, what do you think of the idea?

_____

_____

_____

_____

James says that the result of confessing and being forgiven is being healed (5:16). He's using "healing" here in a metaphorical sense, similar to the way the prophets Isaiah and Jeremiah did. Both prophets used sickness and wounds that need healing as a metaphor for sin. Isaiah 1:4-6, for example, compares the sinfulness of the nation to someone whose head has been injured, whose heart is sick, who is covered in wounds. In Jeremiah 6:13-14 the prophet condemns the cheating and greed of other prophets and priests and says that their refusal to acknowledge the serious problems in the nation of Israel is like superficially attending to a wound (saying, "Peace, peace," when there is no peace). Then in Jeremiah 30:12 he says that Israel's battering by their enemies due to their own sin is like an incurable injury that can't be healed.

Pause a minute to thank God for his forgiveness in your life and the healing change it has brought about in you.

ELIJAH PRAYED

In 5:17-18, James refers to the story of the prophet Elijah found in 1 Kings 17–18. Ahab, the king of Israel, had married a foreigner (Jezebel) and introduced Baal worship (1 Kings 16:29-34). God responded to this evil through his prophet Elijah.

Read 1 Kings 17:1 and 18:1, 16-46. What do you find remarkable about Elijah in this story?

_____

_____

_____

_____

What is James's point in saying that Elijah is someone like us?

_____

_____

_____

_____

IF ONE OF YOU SHOULD WANDER

The image of wandering used in James 5:20 would bring sheep to mind in that part of the ancient world. Read Ezekiel 34:1-6.

What should the shepherds of Israel have done?	What did they do instead?	What happened to the sheep as a result?

Ezekiel assumes it is the responsibility of the shepherds or leaders of Israel to keep the sheep (the people) from wandering. Who, by contrast, does James suggest has this responsibility?

_____

_____

_____

_____

What is the significance of this for your Christian community?

_____

_____

_____

_____

Jesus uses the same metaphor in Matthew 18:12-14. How does this expand our understanding of what James tells us?

_____

_____

_____

_____

Think about someone you know who may have wandered from the faith. Keeping in mind that James clearly doesn't approve of judgmental, harsh, quarrelsome teachers (3:1–4:10), what might be some ways you could connect positively with such a person?

_____

_____

_____

_____

In 5:20 James uses the phrase "cover over a multitude of sins." What does he mean by this? Read Psalm 32:1 and Psalm 85:1-3. What do these passages communicate about sins being "covered"?

_____

_____

_____

_____

When our sins are forgiven, the effects of the Fall of Adam and Eve are reversed. God said that the day they disobeyed would be the day they would die (Genesis 2:16-17). While they did not die physically that day, their sin set the course for physical and spiritual death. But for those who turn to Christ, his forgiveness "[saves] them from death" and his resurrection "covers" their sins (James 5:20). In Christ, death is defeated. As a result, we receive eternal life now and the resurrection of the body in the age to come. Hallelujah!

[1]See Scot McKnight, *The Letter of James,* New International Commentary on the New Testament (Grand Rapids: Eerdmans, 2011), pp. 424-35; and David P. Nystrom, *James,* The NIV Application Commentary (Grand Rapids: Zondervan, 1997), pp. 300-301.
[2]Craig Keener, *The IVP Bible Background Commentary: New Testament* (Downers Grove, IL: InterVarsity Press, 1993), p. 702.
[3]Richard Foster, *Celebration of Discipline* (San Francisco: HarperSanFrancisco, 1998), pp. 148-49.

PART 3. REFLECT
Call the Elders of the Church to Pray

"We would like to come and pray for you. Is that something you would like?"

Doug, a friend of ours for twenty years, had been diagnosed with late-stage lung cancer. He was under forty and had never been a smoker, but the diagnosis came nonetheless. We had had some opportunities to discuss spiritual issues and concerns with him—though not in depth—and we knew he had attended church most of his life; still, we weren't sure if this offer would be outside his comfort zone or not. When Phyllis asked about coming to pray, however, he enthusiastically welcomed the offer.

Our church has a customary practice of praying for healing. If someone is sick, people in the congregation know they can ask the elders to come, just as James 5 recommends. So the two of us had been called on several times to gather with other elders to pray for people with chronic, acute or terminal illnesses.

The situation with Doug was a bit different in that he wasn't a member of our church. But the church was willing to send us and a few others who volunteered. When we arrived, Doug's two teenage children and a few friends were there too. Andy explained that praying for healing was not magic. We do not manipulate God and tell him what to do. We aren't God. He is. Nonetheless, Andy told them, we know that he loves us, cares for us and wants his best for us. So we can come to God confidently with our requests.

He then asked, "What do you sense God doing in your life?" Doug said that despite his shock at the diagnosis and confusion about what to do, God seemed very real, very close in the midst of it all, almost as if he could touch him. Doug also talked about how great his wife, Marie, had been through it all. She was completely focused on his care and well-

being, making calls to doctors as needed and seeing to his needs. We were struck by this, especially, because Doug and Marie's marriage had not always been a close one. They were often distant from and sometimes tense with each other. It seemed that God was already doing healing in their lives.

"I have some oil here," Andy said then. "It's just ordinary olive oil. The New Testament letter of James says that when elders pray for the sick, they should anoint with oil. In the Old Testament oil is a sign of health, of joy and of God's blessing. I'm wondering if you would like us to use just a drop on your forehead to anoint you as we pray."

With a smile Doug said he thought that would be good. Phyllis invited everyone who wanted to pray aloud to do so, but explained that no one had to. She also noted that short, informal sentence prayers would be good; no long speeches to God were necessary. So we gathered around Doug, who was sitting in his favorite chair. Some put a hand on his shoulder or arm. Others just stood nearby. Andy put a drop of oil on his finger and traced the cross on Doug's forehead. And we prayed.

We thanked God for what he was already doing in Doug's life. We thanked God for the many blessings he had given Doug in family and friends and meaningful work. We acknowledged that humanly his situation was very serious, but that God had good things in mind for Doug. We knew we could entrust Doug into God's care, since he loved Doug far more than any of us could. And, knowing that sickness and illness were not God's will, we prayed that God would heal. We also acknowledged that we didn't know why God sometimes broke through barriers to healing and sometimes didn't. These things were mysterious. But we were confident in both God's power and desire to heal. We prayed that as Doug and Marie continued to walk this path, that God would continue to be close to them, close enough to touch.

After about fifteen minutes of prayers and tears, we all stood in a circle and prayed the Lord's Prayer together to conclude. We also hugged and offered some words of comfort to each other. Doug and Marie then invited us all to lunch, which we gladly accepted.

God designed us to be whole people—body, soul and spirit. And God cares about the totality of who we are, not just our spiritual side. He is the one who gave us bodies, after all, and all he made he declared to be good (Genesis 1:31). The health of our bodies matters to him; he knows and cares when we're sick.

Obviously, sickness can have physical causes that require physical treatment—broken arms, infections, disorders. But lifestyle (what and how much we put into our bodies, the amount of exercise we get, where we live, etc.) can also affect health. So can emotional factors like stress at work or in our relationships.

As James reports, sin can be a factor too (which may be connected to our lifestyle choices and our relationships), as can the Accuser, Satan. For example, when Peter told Cornelius about Jesus he described "how he went around doing good and healing all who were under the power of the devil" (Acts 10:38).

Notice, though, that James does not explicitly say that sin causes illness. He is very careful in how he puts it in 5:15, "And the prayer offered in faith will make the sick person well; the Lord will raise them up. If they have sinned, they will be forgiven." *If* the sick person has sinned, says James. So it is entirely possible to be sick and not have an issue of sin to deal with. This suggests that we should be alert to the possibility of a connection, but never presume one. As noted previously, in John 9 Jesus says the man's blindness was not caused by sin. Likewise Job's troubles were

not caused by his sin either.

James 5:15 raises another question for many people: the question of whether prayer—at least a prayer with strong enough faith—*always* results in healing. Certainly sin can be a barrier to answered prayer. James has already covered this in 4:2-3: "You do not have because you do not ask God. When you ask, you do not receive, because you ask with wrong motives, that you may spend what you get on your pleasures." But, as we looked at earlier, Paul tells in 2 Corinthians 12:7-8 how his thorn in the flesh was not healed—something we certainly can't attribute to the apostle's lack of faith.

Some people, related to 5:15, have wrongly taught that we should in faith "act like" we are healed after praying—even if the symptoms remain. This was not the pattern in the New Testament, however. When Jesus healed the paralytic, the man got up and walked (Mark 2:12). When he healed the Gerasene demoniac, the man sat clothed and in his right mind (Mark 5:15). If the symptoms remain, we are not healed. So if the doctor says we still have diabetes, we should take our insulin.

The question of why God doesn't always heal is an immense one. We say God is Creator and Ruler of the world—and yet, given the evidence in Scripture and in our own experience that everyone (good or bad, Christian or not, full of faith or full of fear) does eventually die, obviously there are times when healing does not take place.

What, then, does James mean when he says that "the prayer offered in faith will make the sick person well"? First, he is affirming, as he is throughout 5:13-18, that we should pray; the word *pray* or some form of it is found in every single verse in this section. Second, he is affirming that God can and does heal. Third, he is affirming that God works in concert with our prayers. Fourth, he makes clear that we do not heal. God is the one who "will raise up" the sick person.

James 5:14, in particular, offers some clarification. In that verse James instructs, "Is anyone among you sick? Let them call the elders of the church to pray over them and anoint them with oil in the name of the Lord." What does it mean to anoint "in the name of the Lord"? This is not a magical incantation we utter to somehow force God's hand.

At base, to do something "in the name of" another means to act by the authority or will of someone else. Ambassadors act according to the instructions of their country's leader; they do not have independent authority. So to pray for healing means we must take into account the will of God in the matter.

While we can be confident that God's will for us is to be whole people—body, soul and spirit—we should not be arrogant in assuming we know what God's total will is in particular situations. James strongly cautions against just such presumption in the rich (1:10), in teachers (3:1-2), in merchants (4:13-17) and in landowners (5:1-6). Obviously, though, his warning against pride applies to all of us in whatever we do, including when we pray. We humbly seek God's will, we confidently ask that God's will be done, but we leave it to God to do his will as he pleases, when he pleases.

Doug has his ups and downs emotionally, physically, spiritually. We continue to call him, visit him and pray for him. In all this we hold to our faith in God's love, grace and mercy, now and forever.

What's the main idea in this section?

What is one thing you can act on based on this reading?

PART 4. DISCUSS
Putting It All Together

OPEN

Think about two or three people you care about who are experiencing some illness or difficulty in life. Without naming anyone, share one or two things that you would like to see happen in them.

READ JAMES 5:12-20.

Broken homes, shattered relationships, damaged emotions—we live in a fragmented and hurting society. As we see all the wounded people around us, we long to help, to offer a healing touch. But, although we will spend our lives becoming complete, we will have a hard time helping others unless we are also seeking wholeness ourselves.

In this study James gives us very practical suggestions for becoming whole people and helping others to do the same.

1. How is 5:12 connected to the themes of the tongue (3:1-12) and of patience (5:9-11)?

2. In verses 13-20 what concluding instructions does James give on helping people become more whole physically, emotionally and spiritually?

3. When have you experienced being prayed for or praying for healing for others? Describe your experience.

4. What do you think sin and forgiveness have to do with praying for healing (v. 15)?

5. When would be appropriate times to confess sin to one another and when might it not be appropriate? Explain.

6. What promises about prayer are especially encouraging to you? Why?

7. What did you learn about Elijah in this passage and in the previous parts of this session?

8. How does his story encourage you and motivate you to pray?

9. Much of what James discusses in this final portion of his letter involves the Christian community. What should the community do when someone has wandered from the truth?

10. How would you like to become more involved in the ministry of helping brothers and sisters toward wholeness physically, spiritually or emotionally?

11. How would you like to see your Christian community become more involved in praying for those who are in trouble?

12. What changes have you seen in yourself since you began this study of James?

13. How have you been encouraged by studying the book of James?

Thank God for specific things that you have learned from studying the book of James.

GUIDELINES FOR LEADERS

My grace is sufficient for you.

2 CORINTHIANS 12:9

*I*f leading a small group is something new for you, don't worry. You don't need to be an expert on the Bible or a trained teacher. The discussion guides in part four are designed to facilitate a group's discussion, not a leader's presentation. Guiding group members to discover together what the Bible has to say and to listen together for God's guidance will help them remember much more than a lecture would. Furthermore, the discussion guides are designed to flow naturally. You may even find that the discussions seem to lead themselves! They're also flexible; you can use the discussion guide with a variety of groups—students, professionals, coworkers, friends, neighborhood or church groups. Each discussion takes forty-five to sixty minutes in a group setting.

There are some important facts to know about group dynamics and helpful discussion. The suggestions listed below should equip you to effectively and enjoyably fulfill your role as leader.

PREPARING FOR THE STUDY

1. Ask God to help you understand and apply the passage in your own life. Unless this happens, you will not be prepared to lead others. Pray too for the various members of the group. Ask God to open your hearts to the message of his Word and motivate you to action.

2. Carefully work through parts one, two and three of each session before your group meets. Spend time in meditation and reflection as you consider how to respond.

3. Write your thoughts and responses in the space provided in the study guide. This will help you to express your understanding of the passage clearly and more easily remember significant ideas you want to highlight in the group discussion.

4. It may help to have a Bible dictionary handy. Use it to look up any unfamiliar words, names or places.

5. Reflect seriously on how you need to apply the Scripture to your life. Remember that the group members will follow your lead in responding to the studies. They will not go any deeper than you do.

LEADING THE STUDY

1. At the beginning of your first time together, explain that these studies are meant to be discussions, not lectures. Encourage the members of the group to participate. However, do not put pressure on those who may be hesitant to speak—especially during the first few sessions.

2. Be sure that everyone in your group has a study guide. Encourage the group to prepare beforehand for each discussion by reading the introduction to the guide and by working through the questions in each study.

3. Begin each study on time. Open with prayer, asking God to help the group understand and apply the passage.

4. Discuss the "Open" question before the Bible passage is read. It introduces the

theme of the study and helps group members begin to open up. It can also reveal where our thoughts and feelings need to be transformed by Scripture. Encourage as many members as possible to respond to the "Open" question, and be ready to get the discussion going with your own response.

5. Have a group member read aloud the passage to be studied as indicated in the guide.

6. The study questions are designed to be read aloud just as they are written. You may, however, prefer to express them in your own words.

   Note also that there may be times when it is appropriate to deviate from the discussion guide. For example, a question may have already been answered. If so, move on to the next question. Or someone may raise an important question not covered in the guide. Take time to discuss it, but try to keep the group from going off on tangents.

7. Avoid answering your own questions. An eager group quickly becomes passive and silent if members think the leader will do most of the talking. If necessary, repeat or rephrase the question until it is clearly understood, or refer to the commentary woven into the guide to clarify the context or meaning.

8. Don't be afraid of silence in response to the discussion questions. People may need time to think about the question before formulating their answers.

9. Don't be content with just one answer. Ask, "What do the rest of you think?" or "Anything else?" until several people have given answers to the question.

10. Try to be affirming whenever possible. Especially affirm participation. Never reject an answer; if it is clearly off-base, ask, "Which verse led you to that conclusion?" or again, "What do the rest of you think?"

11. Don't expect every answer to be addressed to you, even though this will probably happen at first. As group members become more at ease, they will begin to truly interact with each other. This is one sign of healthy discussion.

12. Don't be afraid of controversy. It can be very stimulating. If you don't resolve an issue completely, don't be frustrated. Explain that the group will move on and God may enlighten all of you in later sessions.

13. Periodically summarize what the group has said about the passage. This helps to draw together the various ideas mentioned and gives continuity to the study. But don't preach.

14. Conclude your time together with the prayer suggestion at the end of the study, adapting it to your group's particular needs as appropriate. Ask for God's help in following through on the applications you've identified.

15. End on time.

Many more suggestions and helps for studying a passage or guiding discussion can be found in *How to Lead a LifeGuide Bible Study* and *The Big Book on Small Groups* (both from InterVarsity Press/USA).

BIBLIOGRAPHY

Adam, Peter. *Hearing God's Words: Exploring Biblical Spirituality*. New Studies in Biblical Theology. Downers Grove, IL: InterVarsity Press, 2004.

Beale, G. K., and D. A. Carson, eds. *Commentary on the New Testament Use of the Old Testament*. Grand Rapids: Baker Academic, 2007.

Bray, Gerald Lewis, ed. *James, 1-2 Peter, 1-3 John, Jude*. Ancient Christian Commentary on Scripture, edited by Thomas C. Oden. Downers Grove, IL: InterVarsity Press, 2000.

Keener, Craig S. *The IVP Bible Background Commentary: New Testament*. Downers Grove, IL: InterVarsity Press, 1993.

Kidner, Derek. *Psalms 1-72: An Introduction and Commentary*. Tyndale Old Testament Commentary. Downers Grove, IL: InterVarsity Press, 1973.

Longman, Tremper, and Peter Enns, eds. *Dictionary of the Old Testament: Wisdom, Poetry & Writings*. Downers Grove, IL: InterVarsity Press, 2008.

Marshall, I. Howard, A. R. Millard, J. I. Packer and D. J. Wiseman, eds. *New Bible Dictionary*. 3rd ed. Downers Grove, IL: InterVarsity Press, 1996.

Marshall, I. Howard, Stephen Travis and Ian Paul. *Exploring the New Testament, Volume 2: A Guide to the Letters & Revelation*. 2nd ed. Downers Grove, IL: InterVarsity Press, 2011.

Martin, Ralph P., and Peter H. Davids, eds. *Dictionary of the Later New Testament & Its Developments*. Downers Grove, IL: InterVarsity Press, 1997.

McKnight, Scot. *The Letter of James*. New International Commentary on the New Testament. Grand Rapids: Eerdmans, 2011.

Moo, Douglas J. *James: An Introduction and Commentary*. Tyndale New Testament Commentary. Downers Grove, IL: InterVarsity Press, 1987.

Nystrom, David P. *James*. The NIV Application Commentary. Grand Rapids: Zondervan, 1997.

Ryken, Leland, Jim Wilhoit and Tremper Longman, eds. *Dictionary of Biblical Imagery*. Downers Grove, IL: InterVarsity Press, 1998.

Stulac, George M. *James*. IVP New Testament Commentary. Downers Grove, IL: InterVarsity Press, 1993.

Wall, Robert W. "James, Letter of." In *Dictionary of the Later New Testament & Its Developments*. Edited by Ralph P. Martin and Peter H. Davids. Downers Grove, IL: InterVarsity Press, 1997.